How To Books on business and management

Arranging Insurance
Be a Freelance Sales Agent
Buy & Run a Shop
Buy & Run a Small Hotel
Communicate at Work
Conduct Staff Appraisals
Conducting Effective Interviews
Doing Business Abroad
Doing Business on the Internet
Do Your Own Advertising
Do Your Own PR
Employ & Manage Staff
Invest in Stocks & Shares
Keep Business Accounts
Manage a Sales Team
Manage an Office
Manage Computers at Work
Manage People at Work
Managing Budgets & Cash Flows
Managing Meetings
Managing Yourself

Market Yourself
Master Book-Keeping
Master Public Speaking
Mastering Business English
Organising Effective Training
Prepare a Business Plan
Publish a Book
Publish a Newsletter
Raise Business Finance
Sell Your Business
Start a Business from Home
Start Your Own Business
Starting to Manage
Taking on Staff
Understand Finance at Work
Use the Internet
Winning Presentations
Work in an Office
Write a Report
Write Business Letters
Write & Sell Computer Software

Further titles in preparation

The How To series now contains more than 150 titles in the following categories:

Business Basics
Family Reference
Jobs & Careers
Living & Working Abroad
Student Handbooks
Successful Writing

Please send for a free copy of the latest catalogue for full details (see back cover for address).

HowToBooks

BUSINESS BASICS

MANAGING BUDGETS & CASH FLOWS

How to set and achieve financial targets
in an organisation

Peter Taylor

2nd edition

How To Books

By the same author in this series:
How to Keep Business Accounts

Cartoons by Mike Flanagan

British Library Cataloguing in Publication Data
A catalogue record for this book is available from the British Library.

© Copyright 1996 by Peter Taylor.

Published by How To Books Ltd, Plymbridge House, Estover Road, Plymouth PL6 7PZ, United Kingdom. Tel: (01752) 202301. Fax: (01752) 202331.

First edition 1994
Second edition 1996

Note: The material contained in this book is set out in good faith for general guidance and no liability can be accepted for loss or expense incurred as a result of relying in particular circumstances on statements made in the book. The laws and regulations are complex and liable to change, and readers should check the current position with the relevant authorities before making personal or financial arrangements.

Produced for How To Books by Deer Park Productions
Typeset by PDQ Typesetting, Stoke-on-Trent
Printed and bound by The Cromwell Press, Broughton Gifford, Melksham, Wiltshire.

Contents

Illustrations

Preface

to the Second Edition

Modern economic conditions mean that for any business to survive it must plan its destiny. Gone are the days when a business could muddle through and still produce an acceptable profit. **Budgets** are an essential part of this planning process.

In addition, banks and other financial institutions increasingly call for details of the projected **cashflow** and forecast **profit and loss account**.

My aim has been to produce a simple handbook to cut through the jargon often associated with business subjects and to guide you through the steps necessary to prepare a budget and cashflow forecast for your business. I have included plenty of illustrations to help you through this process: they always say that a picture is worth a thousand words!

Obviously the requirements of each reader will be different and unless you have an enormous tome it will be impossible to cover every conceivable problem within this topic. However I hope that this guide will meet the needs of most readers and give others sufficient insight to know when to ask for help from their professional advisors.

My thanks go to all my clients, past and present, for giving me the experience with which to write this book; also to the Royal Bank of Scotland for their permission to reproduce the cash flow statement on pages 82-83.

Peter Taylor

IS THIS YOU?

Manager   Executive

Department head

Business student   Sole trader

Sales manager

Director   Accountant

Works/factory manager

Retailer   Business owner

Transport manager

Head teacher   Hospital manager

Catering manager

Partner   Entrepreneur

College principal

Hotelier   Treasurer

Voluntary work organiser

Business planner   Training officer

Project manager

Team leader   Construction manager

Finance officer

Police officer   Fire officer

Prison governor

Banker   Lawyer

Resort manager

1
Budgets and Cashflows: What are they?

INTRODUCTION

It was a lovely summer afternoon. The bees buzzed lazily from flower to flower and the swallows circled endlessly in the blue sky. Little Philip sat on the steps to his tree house in his garden. He was deep in thought. His aunt had called to see him the previous day and as she left she had pressed two shiny one pound coins into his hand.

Philip immediately wondered how to spend his money. He already had 40p left from his pocket money. He took a piece of paper and started to work out some sums.

Last time he had been shopping with his mum he had seen a model dinosaur that he wanted, but it cost £1.25 — too much for him to pay from his pocket money! Now he thought he could afford it and still have some money left over to buy some crisps, a chocolate bar and a comic. He jotted down the figures (see figure 1).

Philip didn't know it but what he had prepared was a budget so that he could plan how he would spend his cash.

However in dealing with the subject of budgets and cashflows there are some important points to make clear from the start.

WHY PROFIT AND CASH ARE NOT THE SAME

Having cash at the bank and making a profit are not the same thing although to some extent the two are related. Profitable businesses can experience cashflow problems, whilst businesses which are not profitable may temporarily have surplus funds at the bank.

Profit and cashflow are equally important to the business. Only when *both* are properly managed can the business be successful.

money in

	£	p
Aunt Jane	2	-00
Pocket Money		40
	2	- 40

Money Out

Model Dinosaur	1	-25
Crisps		19
Chocolate		54
Comic		35
	2	-33
Left Over		7p

Fig. 1. Philip's budget.

Managing for profit

Profitability comes from two key elements:

- ensuring that your business is earning the correct gross profit on the sale of its product or services *and*

- controlling the level of overhead expenses.

These terms are more fully discussed in chapter 2. Briefly, the gross profit is the sum left from the sales after payment for the cost of the goods sold. Overheads are the other expenses incurred by the business not directly related to the level of activity and the goods sold: instead they relate to the establishment costs and the financing and day to day running of the business.

Managing the cash

Good cashflow is achieved by managing cash resources effectively. Cash management will involve:

- ensuring the business is running profitably — see above

- effective control of debtors — ensuring that you receive payments on time

- taking available credit on purchases

- correct management and financing of capital projects

- getting correct stocking levels to avoid locking up too much capital in stock.

We will return to each of these topics later and discuss how our objectives can be achieved.

Cashflow

Cash is the life-blood of a business. One of the main reasons for business failures is a shortage of cash so that the business simply cannot pay its liabilities as they fall due. More businesses fail as the economy comes out of a recessionary period than during a recession itself. This is because increased trade calls for increased working capital, and may be beyond the means of the business to provide. The cash requirements of a business are very often under-estimated by its managers, but time spent assessing the cash needs of the business will be time well spent.

It will:

- identify times when cash will be in short supply so that you can plan accordingly

- ensure adequate funds are available for capital projects

- allow decisions to be made on a sound basis leading to greater efficiency and increased profits.

But this forecast needs to be based on accurate predictions, in other words a budget.

WHAT IS A BUDGET?

Someone once defined it this way: 'A statement of a financial position for a definite period of time, based on estimates of expenditure and proposals for financing them'. That sounds a bit grand, but it's really quite a simple idea. In young Philip's case his budget was for a very short period, say the afternoon. He had worked out that if he bought the model dinosaur he would still have enough left over to buy the other things that he wanted. He had estimated his total expenditure at £2.33 and since his finance was £2.40, he had a budget surplus of 7p. He had planned his budget and made his decisions accordingly.

Although a budget can be prepared for almost anything from Philip's pocket money to running the country, in business it is generally used to forecast and monitor the business for the year ahead.

The budget is a plan expressed in quantitative terms. Sales are forecast as a number of units sold and the revenue earned is then calculated. The expenses relating to that level of sales must also be calculated. Deduction will be included for overhead expenses which will not be affected by the level of activity. Allowing for all these factors you can then estimate the profit that the business will earn in the coming year. You can also estimate the state of the business finance at the end of the coming year. Note: although we are primarily involved in financial budgeting, resources (labour or machine hours etc) can also be budgeted for.

But why prepare budgets for your business?

There are several reasons for preparing a budget for a business. They include:

- so that you can plan what your business will do

- so that you can monitor the progress of your business

- so that you can manage the various aspects of your business

- to deal with the bank or other financial institution from which you wish to borrow money.

Planning your business

One reason for preparing the budget is so that you can plan the development of your business and make sure that your ideas will work. It would be no use planning to open a second branch of your business if you calculate that the expected sales will not cover the cost of the extra wages. The budget lets you try out your ideas on paper before you put them into practice — it's much less painful on the pocket if you get it wrong!

The budget will also enable you to sell your ideas to your colleagues. Suppose that you thought that by adding a pizzeria to your chip shop business you could increase your profits but to do so will cost £25,000. Your partner in the chip shop may not agree. However if you have done your homework and prepared a realistic budget to show that the additional sales will indeed produce extra profit, even allowing for the cost of the additional finance, then you have won half the battle.

We will discuss the various processes in setting the budget in chapters 4 to 6.

Monitoring the progress of your business

For your own use a budget can be a useful tool to monitor the progress of your business. With the very simplest of businesses you can perhaps manage without such things — if there is money in the bank you must be doing ok! But as the business grows it may acquire more stocks of goods to be resold; it has debtors (money owed to you by customers) and creditors (money you owe to your suppliers). You can no longer check the progress of your business just by looking at your bank statement. Instead you need to prepare a monthly budget showing the way you expect the business to perform; you can then check your actual progress against your target.

We will look at this evaluation process and show you how you can check the progress of your business in chapter 8.

Managing your business
Monitoring the business is only part of the process. You must also act on the matters highlighted by that procedure. If the monitoring shows that you are consistently undercharging for your services, and this is showing losses compared with your budgeted forecast, then you will not achieve the planned profit for the year. You may then decide to review your pricing so as to get the most from your business.

Applying for finance for your business
If you approach a bank for a loan for your business you will often be asked for a budgeted profit and loss account for the next twelve months, plus a balance sheet showing your forecast financial situation at the end of the period. Don't worry if these terms are new to you: we will look at them in more detail in chapter 2. The bank may also ask for a cashflow forecast and once again we will deal with this in more detail later in this book. Most banks have standard forms like the one on page 82 to help you with these tasks.

Is the budget a guess?
The answer is Yes and No! There should always be some valid basis for the inclusion of the figures in the budget — they should not be just a wild guess. We will look at their estimation later on but even with all the information to hand no one can accurately forecast the future and so there is bound to be an element of uncertainty in setting the figures.

SUMMARY

- There is a difference between cash availability and profitability.

- Profitability comes from earning the right rate of gross profit and controlling the level of overheads.

- Good cash management is imperative to the profitable running of the business.

- The importance of the cash availability to the business is just as critical as profitability.

- A budget is a financial plan for the future trading of the business.

- As well as planning the future for the business it is also important to monitor the progress throughout the year.

CASE STUDY

Mike runs a small foundry. His sales for the last two months have been poor due to seasonal factors but he has recently received some good orders which will keep him busy for the months to come. However his creditors are pressing for payment and he has therefore approached his bank for an overdraft. The bank manager has asked to see a budgeted profit and loss account and a cashflow statement. With the help of a friend, Mike has produced these. They show that although he will need additional finance for the next three months, thereafter he will have surplus receipts each month and be able to repay the overdraft by the end of the year. He takes these forecasts to his bank manager who is then happy to allow the overdraft facility.

2
Introducing Business Accounts

THE 'ACCOUNTS'

Like most professions, accountancy has a lot of jargon. Although some of it can be ignored you will need a basic understanding of what is going on. In the last chapter we mentioned establishing a **budgeted profit & loss account** and a **balance sheet** for the business. But what is a profit and loss account or a balance sheet? These documents, together with the accompanying notes, form the **accounts** of the business — a summary of its profit for the period and its financial standing at the end of the period. Normally the profit and loss account will summarise the trading results for a year but it can be prepared for any longer or shorter period of time.

By estimating the future trading activities of the business you can prepare a projected profit and loss account and also forecast the financial position of the business at the end of the period.

There are different ways of setting out year end accounts but the example shown in figure 2 shows one of the most common layouts. This consists of three items:

- a balance sheet

- a profit and loss account

- a schedule of notes expanding on the information shown in the other two documents.

To use an analogy, we could compare the accounts with a flower bed. On 1st July 19X1 you look at the flower bed and although you are quite pleased with it you feel that it could be improved. You take a photograph to record what it looks like. During the next year you work hard on the flower bed, spreading fertilizer, weeding and

ANDREW PHILIPS
BALANCE SHEET
as at 31st March 19X2

	Note	19X2 £	19X1 £
FIXED ASSETS	1.	<u>12644</u>	<u>12097</u>
CURRENT ASSETS			
Stock	2.	30757	26533
Sundry Debtors and Prepayments		–	580
Bank Deposit Account		2512	9622
Bank Account		17	–
Cash in Hand		<u>857</u>	<u>695</u>
		31143	37430
CURRENT LIABILITIES			
Bank Overdraft		–	56
Sundry Creditors and Accruals		<u>4420</u>	<u>6266</u>
		4420	6322
NET CURRENT ASSETS		<u>29723</u>	<u>31108</u>
NET ASSETS		42367	43205
FINANCED BY:			
CAPITAL ACCOUNT	3.	42367	43205

ACCOUNTANTS REPORT
In accordance with instructions given to us, we have prepared these
accounts, without conducting an audit, from the accounting records and
information and explanations supplied to us.

15th July 19X2   Harding Higgins Partnership
                                        Chartered Accountants
                                        Uttoxeter

Fig. 2a. Example accounts – balance sheet.

```
ANDREW PHILIPS
PROFIT AND LOSS ACCOUNT
Year Ended 31st March 19X2

                                              19X2        19X1
                                               £           £

SALES                                         73951       65109


Opening Stock                                 26533       21521
Purchases                                     48883       44102
Closing Stock                                (30757)     (26533)

COST OF SALES                                 44659       39090

GROSS PROFIT                                  29292       26019


Deduct: OVERHEAD EXPENDITURE
    Salaries and Wages                         3833        3599
    Wife's Wages                               1961        1845
    Motor Expenses                              755         802
    Repairs and Renewals                       5910         329
    Telephone Charges                           249         122
    Printing and Stationery                    1155         607
    Heating and Lighting                        646         570
    Insurance                                   725         567
    Rates                                      1524        1392
    Alarm Rental                                604         509
    Hire Purchase Interest                      111           -
    Bank Interest and Charges                   179         445
    Discount Allowed                            289         272
    Professional Fees                             -          13
    Accountancy Charges                         365         350
    Sundry Expenses                             604         541
    Depreciation                    1.         1398        1216
    Loss on Sale of Assets          1.          881           -
                                              21189       13179

NET TRADING PROFIT                             8103       12840

Add: Sundry Income - Bank Interest             190         277

NET PROFIT FOR THE YEAR                        8293       13117
```

Fig. 2b. Example accounts – profit & loss account.

ANDREW PHILIPS
NOTES TO THE ACCOUNTS
Year Ended 31st March 19X2

1. FIXED ASSETS

	Written down value beginning of year	Additions	Sale proceeds	Dep'n for year	Written down value end of year
Freehold Property	8448	-	-	-	8448
Motor Vehicles	3381	4000	(2500)	(1000)	
				* (881)	3000
Furniture & Fittings	268	1326	-	(398)	1196
	12097	5326	(2500)	2279	12644

* Loss on Sale

Depreciation has been charged at the following rates:

Freehold Property	Nil	
Motor Vehicles	25%	On Book Value
Furniture & Fittings	25%	On Book Value

2. STOCK
    Stock has been valued at the lower of cost or net realisable value.

3. CAPITAL ACCOUNT   £
    As at 1st April 19X1   43205
    Profit for the year   8293
    Drawings   (9131)
                                           42367

4. Taxation
    No provision has been made in these accounts in respect of taxation.

Fig. 2c. Example accounts – notes to the accounts.

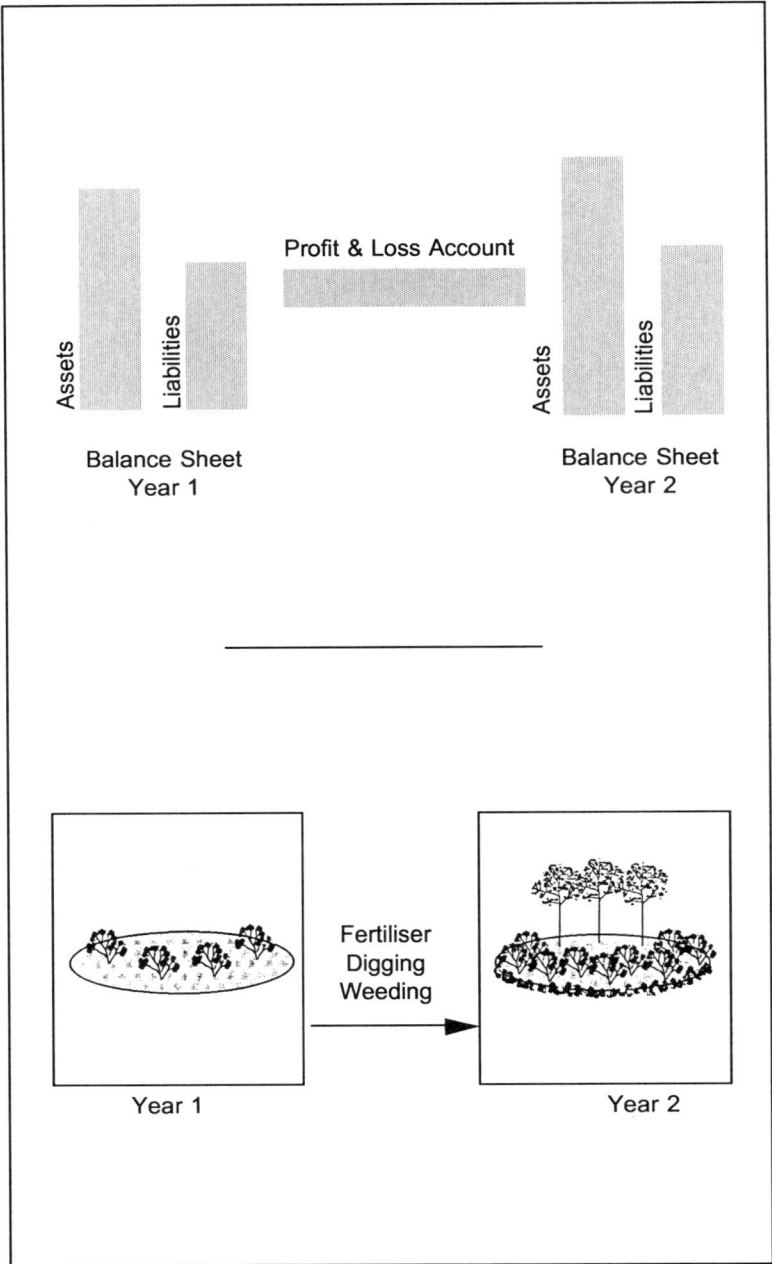

Fig. 3. The 'flower bed example'.

digging, and in the spring you plant out some bedding plants. You also visit the local garden centre and purchase some extra plants. The year comes round and on the 1st July 19X2 you are out in your garden again looking at the flower bed. Yes, it really does look different so you take another photograph to record what it now looks like.

But what has this to do with accountancy? Well the photographs are like a balance sheet — they record what there is in the flower bed at a point in time. A balance sheet is a 'financial snapshot' which records the assets and liabilities of the business at a moment in time. And all the digging and weeding and the extra plants can be likened to the trading of the business during the year, which would be recorded on the profit and loss account.

Let's look at them each in turn.

The balance sheet

As explained above, the first page of the accounts, the **balance sheet**, is a 'snapshot' of the business at a point in time. It shows the **assets** and **liabilities** of the business at that moment. Assets are all the things that belong to the business (amounts invested in bank accounts, book debts and stock, as well as buildings, equipment and motor vehicles). Liabilities are the amounts owed by the business to others; as well as amounts owed for goods purchased (creditors) liabilities include bank overdrafts and loans.

Year end accounts usually also show the figures for the previous year, so that the reader can easily see how the values have changed during the year. Is more money invested in stock, or less? Has the business reduced or increased its creditors?

When looking at a budgeted balance sheet it would be usual to have actual figures from the latest accounts in one column and the projected figures in the other column.

Profit and loss account

The second page, the **profit and loss account**, is a summary of the trading income and expenditure for the period; it shows the way in which the business has traded. It 'reconciles' the movements of assets and liabilities between the two balance sheet dates. Once again it is common practice to show comparative figures on year end accounts. When dealing with budgeted profit and loss accounts it is often useful to split the transactions into monthly periods. In this way it is easier to monitor the actual progress of the business compared with the budget and it is also possible to build into the model of the business the seasonal trends.

KEY RATIOS TO LOOK OUT FOR

As well as an analytical comparison of one year with the next to see how the business has developed there are often some **key ratios** to consider in appraising the development of the business. These might include:

The gross profit margin

The **gross profit** is the profit from trading after allowing for the direct costs (the purchase of goods and manufacturing labour) but before deducting overhead expenses. It is useful to compare the rate of profit (normally as a percentage of sales) from one year to the next to ensure that the profit margins on the sales of goods are being maintained. In this way you can see how much profit is being earned on each £1 of sales.

The net profit margin

While the gross profit ignores the overhead costs, the **net profit** takes account of all costs. It is the final 'bottom line' figure on the profit and loss account. The **net profit margin** relates this profit to sales again as a percentage. It is less important than the gross profit margin as it is more relevant to look at the actual **figures** of profit rather than the profit **rate**.

Stock turnover rate

The stock turnover rate can be a good indication of the level of stock that a business should carry. It will vary from one industry to another. Businesses in like trades might be expected to have a similar rate of stock turnover. The stock turnover rate is the number of times that a business can sell its stock during a year; you calculate it by dividing the annual turnover by the value of the stock on hand at the year end. If for example you are running a sandwich shop then you need to have a very high stock turnover rate. Who can sell a sandwich which is weeks old! On the other hand a hardware shop would be likely to have a low stock turnover rate because there are so many different lines of stock, each of them slow moving, and none of them perishable.

· CAPITAL EXPENDITURE AND REVENUE EXPENDITURE

Before we go further there is an important distinction to be made between two types of expenditure in a business:

- **Capital expenditure** means the purchase of fixed assets which will be used by the business and have a lasting effect for several years.

- **Revenue expenditure** on the other hand only contributes once towards the earning of profits. Except for any items which remain as stock, revenue expenditure is wholly used up in the period that the expenditure is incurred.

Example

So for example, expenditure on a new machine to be used by the business for the manufacture of its products or the cost of a new building would be capital. This expenditure should benefit the business for several years. Expenditure on the raw materials purchased to make the product to be sold by the business, the cost of wages or expenditure on motor expenses would be classified as revenue expenditure. These will have no long term advantage and their benefit will be 'used up' in the same accounting period as the expenditure.

Revenue income and capital income

In the same way income can be classified into revenue and capital. If a building that has been used by the business as a warehouse for several years is sold for a profit then this is a **capital** profit. Alternatively, when the business sells the goods that it has manufactured as its trade then this is **revenue** income.

Broadly the profit and loss account and the balance sheet follow this same division. Items that have a *lasting* benefit (and are therefore *capital*) will appear on the balance sheet, whereas revenue items will appear on the profit and loss account. But what about items such as stock or trade debtors? Although these assets are not of a capital nature their benefit *does* carry forward from one accounting period to the next. They will therefore show up on our 'snapshot' of the business at the year end and be included on the balance sheet. It's the same with creditors (amounts owed by the business). These liabilities which are of a revenue nature again carry forward from one accounting period to the next and will appear on the balance sheet. For more detail on the exact double entry involved you should consult a book on accounting such as *How to Keep Business Accounts* in this series.

THE TYPICAL BALANCE SHEET

As we have seen, the balance sheet shows the values of the capital assets and those revenue items such as stocks which are on hand and carry forward from one period to the next. But the balance sheet is not just a jumbled list of these figures. It is normally sorted into an order so that the reader can easily establish the financial strength of the business. If you look at figure 2 you will see the various categories of items.

Fixed assets

These are the capital assets such as buildings, machines, vans that are going to have a lasting benefit to the business. This class can be subdivided into **tangible** and **intangible** fixed assets. Generally tangible fixed assets are items that you can go and kick — a building, machine etc. Intangible fixed assets include goodwill: although it is hoped that it will have a lasting benefit to the business there is nothing physical about goodwill (or other intangibles) that you can see or touch.

Example

Fixed assets	£
Freehold property	8,448
Motor vehicles	3,000
Furniture & fittings	1,196
	12,644

Current assets

This means the other non-capital class of assets of the business. It includes stock, debtors, money in the bank or cash in hand. These assets are essentially short term in nature (less than one year). They are either cash or can readily be converted into cash. By convention the least liquid (most remote from cash) is listed first, then you work through in order to cash itself.

Current assets include revenue items carried forward from one accounting period to the next. As mentioned above this will include both stock and debtors.

Example

Current assets	£
Stock	30,757
Sundry Debtors & Prepayments	492
Bank Deposit Account	2,037
Cash in Hand	857
	34,143

Current liabilities

This category includes amounts owed to suppliers etc (creditors) and short term financing such as a bank overdraft. Once again, like current assets above, current liabilities will include revenue items which are owing at the end of the accounting period.

Example

Current liabilities	£
Bank Overdraft	274
Sundry Creditors & Accruals	4,146
	4,420

Net current assets

This total is the difference between the current assets and the current liabilities of the business. It is also sometimes referred to as the **working capital** — the value available to the business for its day to day running. Often when a business expands rapidly it needs extra working capital to pay suppliers, and to lock up in extra stock. If the business is unable to generate this additional working capital it can run into financial difficulties.

Example

Net Current Assets	
Current Assets	34,143
Current Liabilities	4,420
	29,723

Long term liabilities

This heading will include items of long term finance (bank loans or hire purchase) which have more than one year to go before repayment. Because of their nature such liabilities do not appear on all balance sheets.

Net assets

This total is the difference between the assets and the liabilities of the business. This figure shows the net worth of the business.

Example

Fixed Assets	12,644
Net Current Assets	29,723
	42,367

Remember that the figure for net current assets is after the deduction of current liabilities. You must also adjust for long term liabilities if applicable.

Proprietor's investment

The net assets are matched by an equal and opposite figure — the **proprietor's investment** in the business. This may have been money actually invested in the business or it may represent profits earned by the business and not withdrawn. Either way it represents the money owed by the business to the owner: if all the assets were sold and all the liabilities paid then this sum could be paid by the business to its owner.

THE TYPICAL PROFIT & LOSS ACCOUNT

The balance sheet was a snapshot of the business at a specified point in time. The profit and loss account shows the *movements* of values during a specified **accounting period**, eg a year. What is an accounting period? It can be any period required. The profit and loss account can be prepared for any period of time: a week, a month, a quarter, six months or a year. Normally the profit and loss account will be prepared at least once a year; we will assume from now on that you are preparing annual accounts.

The profit and loss account summarises the revenue income and expenditure that took place during the year. Allowances are made for timing differences (debtors and creditors) and an adjustment is made for the stock on hand at the end of the year. The result is that the account displays the *net* result of the trading during the year, showing how much profit or loss has been made.

If you look at figure 2 you will see that the report is split into two main sections. These are:

- The **trading account** — this part of the report shows the **gross profit** and how it has been calculated.

- The **overheads** — those costs of the business which are not directly related to the level of trade. Even if the business had no sales it would still incur some overheads such as rent, rates, insurance and perhaps wages.

The **gross profit** is the difference between the value at which goods have been sold by the business and the cost of those goods. (Where a business is carrying out a service — for example a solicitor — it would be inappropriate to try to calculate a gross profit and in such circumstances the report would be modified and would appear as in figure 4.)

```
ANDREW PHILIPS
PROFIT AND LOSS ACCOUNT
Year Ended 31st March 19X2


                                          19X2        19X1
                                            £           £

SALES                                     73951       65109


Deduct: EXPENDITURE
  Purchases                               48883       44102
  Stock Movement During Year     2.       (4224)      (5012)
  Salaries and Wages                       3833        3599
  Wife's Wages                             1961        1845
  Motor Expenses                            755         802
  Repairs and Renewals                     5910         329
  Telephone Charges                         249         122
  Printing and Stationery                 1155         607
  Heating and Lighting                      646         570
  Insurance                                 725         567
  Rates                                    1524        1392
  Alarm Rental                              604         509
  Hire Purchase Interest                    111          -
  Bank Interest and Charges                 179         445
  Discount Allowed                          289         272
  Professional Fees                          -           13
  Accountancy Charges                       365         350
  Sundry Expenses                           604         541
  Depreciation                    1.       1398        1216
  Loss on Sale of Assets          1.        881          -
                                          65848       52269

Add: Sundry Income - Bank Interest         190         277

                                          65658       51992

NET PROFIT FOR THE YEAR                    8293       13117
```

Fig. 4. Example accounts — profit & loss account
— no gross profit shown.

ACCOUNTING FOR DEPRECIATION

Another issue to consider in the preparation of the accounts is
depreciation. As we have seen **fixed assets** are those items having a
lasting value to the business: a motor van, a piece of machinery, or

some office furniture. But even these items will not last for ever. Over the years they will lose value and the accounts should reflect this.

To deal with this it is normal to 'write off' part of the value of the asset each year as an expense of the business: that is to *depreciate* it. It is not normally practical (or necessary) to obtain an actual valuation of the assets each year to see how much value has been lost. Instead, the proprietor of the business will have a fairly good idea of the life of the asset. From this he can calculate how much to transfer from the asset account and treat as an expense in the profit and loss account to reflect the value lost during the year.

There are two main methods of working out depreciation:

- the straight line method
- the reducing balance method

The choice is up to the individual and will depend partly on the nature of the asset and partly on personal preference. However, whichever system is adopted it should be applied *consistently* from year to year; the method and rates should *not* be changed without good reason.

Straight line depreciation
Under this method the cost of the asset is written off by equal amounts each time. By the end of its expected life its value will have been reduced to the anticipated **residual** value.

Example
A motor van was purchased for £4000. It was expected that after four years of service to the business it would be sold for £1200. Over the four years it would therefore have lost value by £2800, or £700 per year. Each year the van would be 'depreciated' by £700 and this amount would appear as an expense in the profit and loss account.

Reducing balance method
This method reduces the value of the asset by a fixed rate each year based on the diminishing value. The rate used should be such that the depreciation is roughly equal to the loss in value over the period of use.

Example
Using the same example as above, if the van was depreciated at 25%

per annum the result would be:

	£
Van – cost	4000
Yr 1: Depreciation 25% x £4000 =	1000
Reduced value at end of year 1	3000
Yr 2: Depreciation 25% x £3000 =	750
Reduced value at end of year 2	2250
Yr 3: Depreciation 25% x £2250 =	562
Reduced value at end of year 3	1688
Yr 4: Depreciation 25% x £1688 =	422
Reduced value at end of year 4	1266

As you can see, under this system the depreciation is higher in the early years of the ownership and tails off as the asset gets older. This often reflects the pattern of true loss of value of assets – a new car loses a considerable value as soon as it is driven out of the showroom but loses less value in later years.

Example of a 'non-cash' expense

Lastly on this topic, depreciation is unlike most other expenses in the profit and loss account in that it does not involve any movement of cash. When you purchase goods or services there is always a payment of cash to record this, but depreciation is only an accounting entry to ensure that the loss of value of the asset is reflected in the profit and loss account during the period incurred. This distinction will be important when we consider the **cashflow forecast** (chapter 7).

WHAT 'ACCOUNTING CONCEPTS' MEAN

Before we leave the subject of the preparation of the accounts we should also mention the **Accounting Concepts**. There are four Accounting Concepts used in business:

- the Going Concern concept
- the Accruals concept
- the Consistency concept
- the Prudence concept.

The going concern concept

This concept states that you must treat the business as a going concern when you are preparing the accounts, unless there is some very clear pointer to show that this would be incorrect. The importance of this is mainly to do with the valuation of stock or other assets of the business; apart from this brief outline it is a topic that is beyond the scope of this book.

The accruals concept

To **accrue** in accountancy terms means to charge an expense (or to take income) in the period in which it was incurred or earned — *regardless of when the payment is actually made*. Suppose a business makes up its accounts to 31st December and during December it purchases goods on credit which are paid for in January; the value of the goods is charged as an expense in *December* even though the invoice for the goods has not yet been paid. The *liability* to pay for the goods will be shown as a creditor on the balance sheet.

The accruals concept also covers expenses which, though settled by one payment, have a benefit which may go beyond the end of the accounting period. Suppose for example the above mentioned business pays its rent every six months (in arrears) on 30th September and 31st March. At 31st December the business will owe three months rent (October – December); even though the rent has not actually become due for payment the business has had the use of the premises. An adjustment ('accrual') should be made in the accounts to reflect this.

The accruals concept is very important and as we will see later forms a major contrast between the profit and loss account and the cashflow forecast.

The consistency concept

This simply means that matters within the accounts should be treated in a similar manner each year. The goalposts, as it were, should not be moved. For example depreciation rates should be the same each year.

The prudence concept

Don't assume a profit until it is actually earned! Always be prudent and err on the side of caution. If goods have been sold on credit then (using the accruals concept) you can state the profit on the sale, even though the goods have not yet been paid for. But if there is any suggestion that the debt may not be paid, you must provide for the potential loss that may arise from the transaction.

CONCLUSION

The above has been a quick summary of the preparation of business accounts. We have covered the following topics:

- The contents of the year end accounts
- Gross profit
- Net profit
- Capital and revenue expenses
- Depreciation
- Accounting concepts

DISCUSSION POINTS

Which of the following are **revenue** expenses and which are **capital** expenses:

(a) The purchase of a new delivery van for the business.
(b) The payment for the telephone bill.
(c) The repainting of the outside of the factory.
(d) The purchase of materials to be used in the production process of the business.
(e) Salary payments for office staff.
(f) The purchase of a new warehouse to store the finished products from the production process of the business.

Answer:

The following are revenue expenses - b, c, d, and e. Items a, and f, are capital expenses.

3
Managing VAT

In the last chapter we looked at some of the key points in the preparation of accounts so that we could tackle the preparation of the budget. However before we look at the budget there is a further matter to consider — VAT. Almost everyone running a business will be affected by VAT in one way or another, so here is a quick summary to put it in context.

REGISTERING FOR VAT

Should I be registered for VAT?

It depends upon your turnover. If your **taxable supplies** (ie those sales not exempted from VAT — see later) exceed £47,000 in any twelve month period then you must register for VAT. You have to send notification that your business exceeded the limit to the Customs & Excise (who administer the tax) within 30 days of the end of the month in which the turnover exceeded the limit. Registration will then take place from the first day of the following month.

If your turnover is below the limit for compulsory registration you may still apply for VAT registration if you think that it will be advantageous. For example if you are selling most of your products to other businesses which are themselves VAT registered then it will probably be best for you to register. Why? — because you will then be able to recover the **input tax** on your purchases; although you will have to charge VAT to your customers, they will of course be able to get the tax back again (assuming they in turn are registered).

What if I decide not to register?

If you do not have to apply for compulsory registration for VAT, and you also decide not to register on a voluntary basis, then you will still find that you have VAT charged to you on your purchases. However, since you cannot recover the VAT then there is no need to separate it from the cost of the goods or services bought by the business. Just treat the amount that you actually pay as the cost of the goods.

So I've got to register — how does VAT work?

Under VAT, every business is effectively a tax collector. The tax is charged on the sale of goods or services by each business which is registered for VAT (except that certain transactions are exempt from VAT or are charged at a zero rate: more about that on page 38). On most other transactions the rate of VAT is currently 17.5% of the price of the goods. This rate is referred to as the **Standard Rate.** Since 1st April 1994 VAT has been chargeable on domestic fuel (for heating: not road fuel) at 8% but subjected to standard rate VAT for most commercial concerns. All the transactions which attract VAT at either standard rate or zero rate are called **taxable supplies**; the VAT charged out to your customers is called **output tax**.

On the other hand, when your registered business buys goods or services from another registered supplier then you must pay an amount of VAT charged to you by that business. This tax on goods coming *into* your business is called **input tax**.

You will have to settle up with the Customs & Excise at the end of your VAT period — normally once a month or once a quarter. If the total of your output tax (on sales) exceeds the total of the input tax on your purchases (as is usually the case) then you must pay the difference to the VAT office. If your input tax exceeds your output tax then you can claim a refund.

Why is it called Value Added Tax?

That's easy — it's because the net effect of this set-off of input and output tax is to levy a tax on *the value added*. Consider the following:

Example
Suppose a shop buys a shirt from a wholesaler for £6.00 (plus VAT): the payment to the wholesaler is therefore £7.05. The shop then sells the shirt for £11.75 (£10.00 + £1.75 VAT). The transaction can be summarised thus:

	Goods	*VAT*	
	£ p	£ p	
Sale	10.00	1.75	(output tax)
Purchase	6.00	1.05	(input tax)
Difference	4.00	0.70	

You will see that the shop has added £4.00 to the value of the shirt — this is the 'valued added' bit (remember that we are only looking at the goods value — not the total price paid). The tax on the *value added* is £4.00 x 17.5% = £0.70.

To see this another way refer to figure 5.

What if the invoice doesn't show VAT separately?

This sometimes happens, particularly on smaller purchases such as the purchase of petrol from a garage. Remember, the invoice must show the supplier's VAT number if you are to reclaim the VAT. Subject to certain restrictions, the supplier can issue a 'less detailed tax invoice' in such cases.

Beware when this happens. Many people work out the VAT incorrectly as follows:

Petrol invoice   £10.00
  VAT content £10.00 x 17.5% = £1.75

This is wrong!

The amount paid for the petrol is *inclusive* of the VAT. Thus if you say that the cost of the petrol (excluding VAT) is 100% of the net value (ie, it is the net value) then the VAT charge will be 17.5% of the net value. And so the total cost represents 100% + 17.5% = 117.5% of the net value. Therefore from this we can work out that the VAT content is:

$$\frac{17.5\%}{117.5\%} \text{ x total invoice value}$$

So the VAT on our £10.00 of petrol is only £1.49, not £1.75.

You should also note that the fraction can be 'simplified' to 7/47ths of the total price to reveal the VAT content, but as this is not very simple simplification let's hope you have a pocket calculator!

ACCOUNTING FOR VAT

As explained above you must notify the VAT office of your inputs and outputs on your VAT return at the end of each VAT period — generally every three months. However, which items do you include on the VAT return? The answer is that it depends. There are two

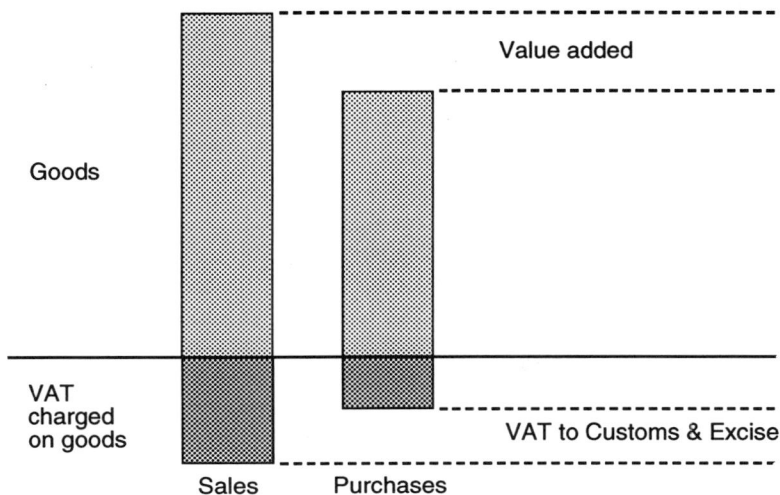

Fig. 5. How VAT works.

alternative systems for accounting for VAT:

- the tax point system
- the cash accounting scheme

The tax point system
This is the normal system. Under this scheme the time that you must account for VAT is fixed by the time of supply, or the tax point as it is known. So the VAT must be accounted for in the VAT period that the goods (or services) are sold regardless of the time that the invoice is actually paid. If goods are sold on credit then you may have to pay the VAT output tax to the Customs & Excise before you receive payment from the customer. Conversely, you may be able to reclaim the VAT on your purchases before you have to pay your supplier for the goods.

The cash accounting scheme
Under this system you only account for the VAT at the time that the cash transaction takes place. If you purchase goods on credit you are not permitted to reclaim the VAT input tax until you actually pay for the goods. In a similar way, there is no need for you to account for VAT output tax on your sales until you have actually received

payment from your customers.

The **cash accounting** basis is only available to businesses whose annual turnover is less than £350,000 — if it is more than this then you must use the normal tax point system.

Which scheme should I choose?

The choice of scheme is dependent on your trading pattern and it can have significant cashflow consequences. If you buy items on credit but sell the goods for cash then you would be unwise to select the cash accounting basis. If you did you would have to wait until you paid for the goods before you could claim your input tax, but you would have to pay the output tax as soon as the sale was made.

If on the other hand you buy goods for cash but sell on credit — or where you are providing a service (eg a painter and decorator) — then it is best to adopt the cash accounting basis if available. By doing so you can claim your input tax as soon as you pay for the goods (in the case of the service business there will be very little input tax) but you will not have to account for the VAT output tax until you receive payment yourself.

Should I always charge VAT at the standard rate?

No. Although most sales carry VAT at the standard rate there are a few items which attract VAT at a **zero rate**. The main categories are:

- food
- books and newspapers (but not stationery)
- land and buildings (but not repairs or extensions to existing property)
- transport of passengers
- certain clothing and footwear (mainly children's).

Except for the fact that the items are charged to VAT at a zero rate (and remember that a number x zero% = zero and therefore there is no VAT actually payable) they are treated in all other ways the same as the standard rated items.

There are also a few items which are **exempt** from VAT: these include insurance, some bank charges and rates. These items are not 'taxable supplies'.

FITTING VAT INTO BUDGETS AND CASH FLOWS

Question — What's the effect of VAT on budgets and cashflows?

Answer — Quite a lot. Before you can prepare your budget, and more particularly your cashflow forecast, you must have a clear understanding of the effect of VAT on the business. For the purpose of setting the budget, assuming that you have registered for VAT, you need only concern yourself with the *net* cost of the goods (ie excluding VAT). You do *not* include the VAT in any of your figures. However when you are preparing the cashflow forecast then it is most important that you do correctly take account of VAT. With VAT at 17.5% you can easily be a long way out if you ignore VAT or treat it wrongly, perhaps with disastrous results. We will see how VAT should be incorporated into the cashflow statement in chapter 7.

SUMMARY

- VAT stands for Value Added Tax — a tax on consumer spending.

- The VAT system collects tax on the value added to the goods by each registered person handling them.

- You must register for VAT if your turnover (sales) exceeds the prescribed limit, but you can register if your turnover is less than the limit if you want.

- Some sales are zero rated.

- Some items are exempted from VAT.

- If your turnover is less than £350,000 you can adopt the 'cash accounting basis' if you want.

- Since VAT can make a material difference to the figures on your cashflow statement, its effects must not be overlooked.

4
Introducing Budgets

PLANNING YOUR WAY AHEAD

In chapter 2 we looked at some of the details of how to prepare accounts for a business. However this was from a *historical* viewpoint: the figures were showing what *had* happened.

In *budgeting* we want to forecast what is *going to happen* and see the financial implications. We can then use this forecast to plan the way that the business will develop in the future.

When the builder is going to erect a house he doesn't just order the bricks and cement and start building. Instead, plans are drawn up so that he has a good idea of what the finished result will look like before he has even started to dig out the foundations.

So it should be in business. The forecast budget is the set of financial plans used to build the business. As with the builder, you may have to modify some details as you progress. The builder may find that soil conditions require deeper foundations than originally planned. The businessman may find that material prices change, so that he must rework his figures to take this into account.

As we have seen a profit and loss account shows the result of trading and can cover any period from one day to one year or more. However, for budgeting to be a useful tool to assist the business it is normal to split the trading into monthly periods.

By forecasting the income and expenditure for the business you can also forecast the balance sheet showing the financial state of affairs of the business in six or twelve months' time.

The preparation of the budget can be as detailed as you require. For example many people just say to themselves. 'I had sales of £87,000 last year. This year I want 10% more, so my sales budget for the year is £96,000.' And often this approach is quite adequate. It will not give you the same clear insight into how your business works, but if you want to take this approach you can skip the rest of this chapter and also chapters 5 and 6.

I hope that most of you will continue to read on. If you work through the budget process it will teach you much about your business. This in turn will put you in a much stronger position to make successful management decisions.

LINKS IN THE BUDGETING CHAIN

The creation of a detailed budget involves an interlinked process as shown in figure 6. Some of the links which will affect the budget are discussed below:

Sales budget ←→ production budget

You will need to consider the production capacity when setting the sales budget. It will be no good forecasting sales of your product at 5000 per week if you can only make 3000. Likewise the productive budget will be affected by the sales budget. Where there is a mix of products being made their relative sales volumes may affect production methods employed.

Sales budget ←→ cost of sales

Once again there are close links between these two budgets. For example, it will be no good setting the selling price of the goods at such a level that it is below the cost of producing the item, and you lose money on every item sold. But you also need an idea of the sales volume when setting the purchases budget (which forms part of the cost of sales) because this may influence the buying price due to quantity discounts etc.

Overheads ←→ sales budget

The overheads of the business will be incurred almost whatever the level of turnover. However the cost of the overheads will need to be carried by the sales of the product. Consider the following:

Example
Overheads = £20,000.

Sales volume	Overhead cost per item £ p
5,000	4.00
10,000	2.00
20,000	1.00
40,000	0.50
60,000	0.33
80,000	0.25
100,000	0.20

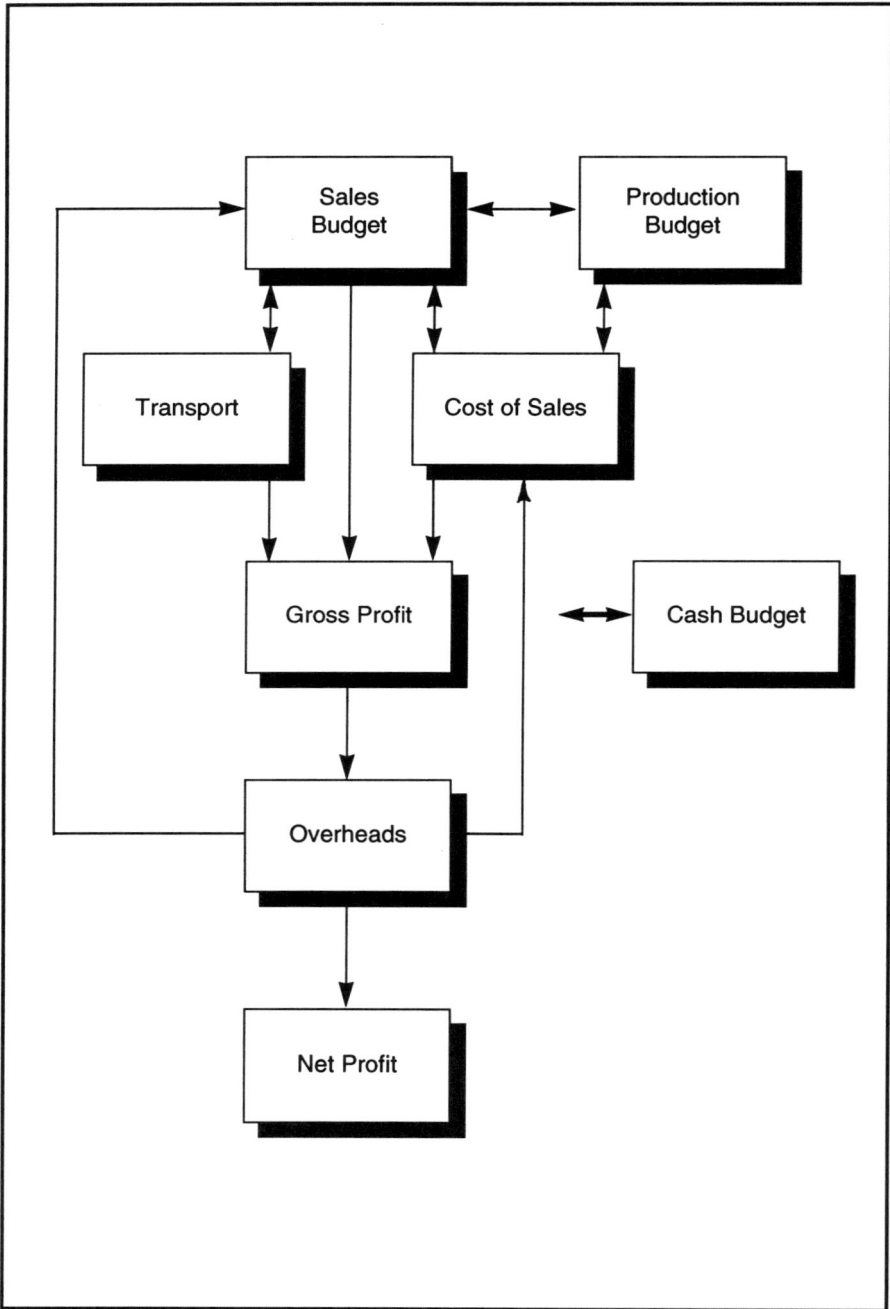

Fig. 6. Linking the elements of the overall business budget.

Clearly the lower the volume of sales the more overhead cost has to be absorbed in the selling price of each item.

In the same way, the transport budget will be affected by the volume and geographical location of sales. For example, how many vans and drivers do you need, or should you use carriers? In practice the overhead expenses are often apportioned back to the cost of sales on a cost centre basis (see the next chapter).

BUDGETING FOR PROFIT

All these elements grouped together enable you to establish the budgeted gross and net profits for the period. With so many links, good communication and cooperation is needed between the various departments drawing up the budget. There will need to be adjustments made to refine the budget so that the different departmental budgets fit together like a jigsaw to form the coordinated overall budget. And the budget will need to be 'fine tuned' to maximise profit.

In a small business this liaison will be easy to achieve: *you* will do all the work! However in a larger organisation even this plan of how to draw up the budget will be quite complex. Figure 7 shows the timetable for drawing up a budget for a private hospital group. You will see that this process is planned to take from 23rd April until 27th October to draw up and approve the annual budget! Figure 8 shows the budget approval process for the same hospital group.

The impact of cash flow

BUT one thing may override all of the carefully worked out departmental budgets discussed above — the **cash budget**. It is no use planning to increase the production and sell three times as many items if the cash is not available to permit such expansion. Remember, the greater turnover would involve more cash tied up in equipment, in stock, and in debtors; unless these funds are available from the cash budget then the plan simply won't become reality. It's then 'back to the drawing board' to revise the figures to a plan which can be funded.

We will look at the cash budget in more detail when we consider **cashflow statements** in chapter 7.

Budgeting for short term fluctuations

One further point is that although you may be drawing up the budget for a twelve month period, that is a *long* time in business.

Timetable for 19XI Business Review, Profit Plan and Capital Expenditure Budget

Week Ended Date

1 Business Review
Phase 1 – Preliminary preparation
Phase 2 – Activity forecasting:
    Submission of preliminary hospital forecast to head office
      Head office review of forecast activity
        Hospitals fine tune and re-submit forecast of activity
        Head office approve forecast of activity

2 Capital Expenditure Budget
Preparation of capital expenditure budget by hospitals
    Submission of hospital capital expenditure budgets to head office
      Head office review of preliminary capital expenditure budgets
        Hospitals fine tune or re-work and re-submit capital budgets
          Head office receive final capital budgets
            Board approval of capital expenditure budget

3 Profit Plan
Head office approval of cost & price assumptions and performance targets
  Board approval of cost & price assumptions and performance targets
    Hospitals advised of targets and cost & price assumptions
      Activity assumptions confirmed to hospitals
        Evaluation of activity budgets and development of expenditure budget
          Submission of full provisional 19XI profit plan to head office
            Head office review of provisional 19XI profit plan
            Hospitals fine tune profit plan and re-submit
              Board meeting to approve 19XI profit plan

Fig 7. Timetable for drawing up a budget.

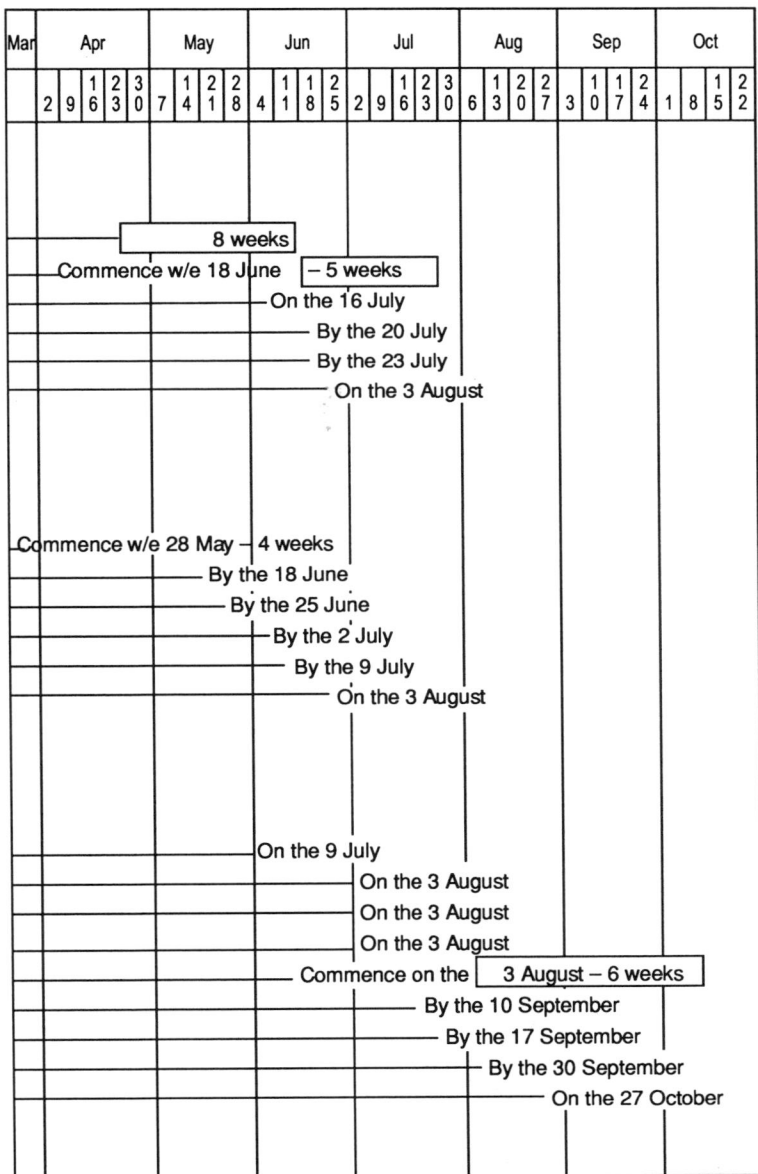

Mar	Apr				May				Jun				Jul					Aug				Sep				Oct			
2	9	16	23	30	7	14	21	28	4	11	18	25	2	9	16	23	30	6	13	20	27	3	10	17	24	1	8	15	22

8 weeks

Commence w/e 18 June — 5 weeks

On the 16 July

By the 20 July

By the 23 July

On the 3 August

Commence w/e 28 May — 4 weeks

By the 18 June

By the 25 June

By the 2 July

By the 9 July

On the 3 August

On the 9 July

On the 3 August

On the 3 August

On the 3 August

Commence on the 3 August — 6 weeks

By the 10 September

By the 17 September

By the 30 September

On the 27 October

Fig 7. Timetable for drawing up a budget.

Budget Approval Process

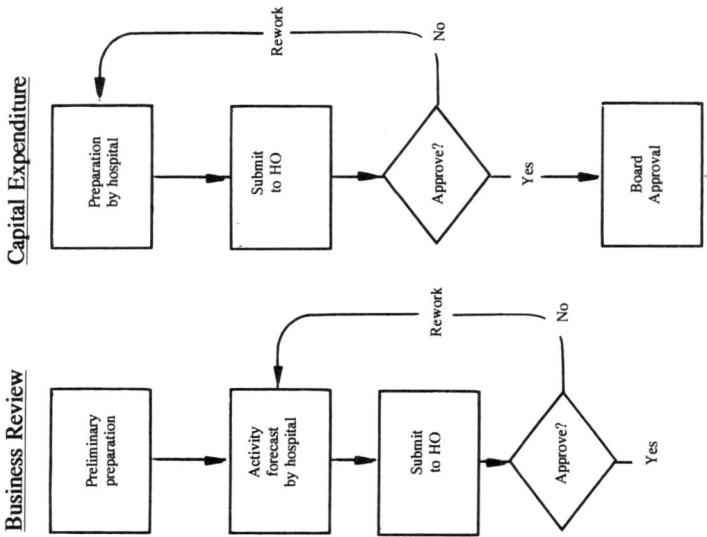

Capital Expenditure

Business Review

Fig. 8. The budget approval process.

Profit Plan

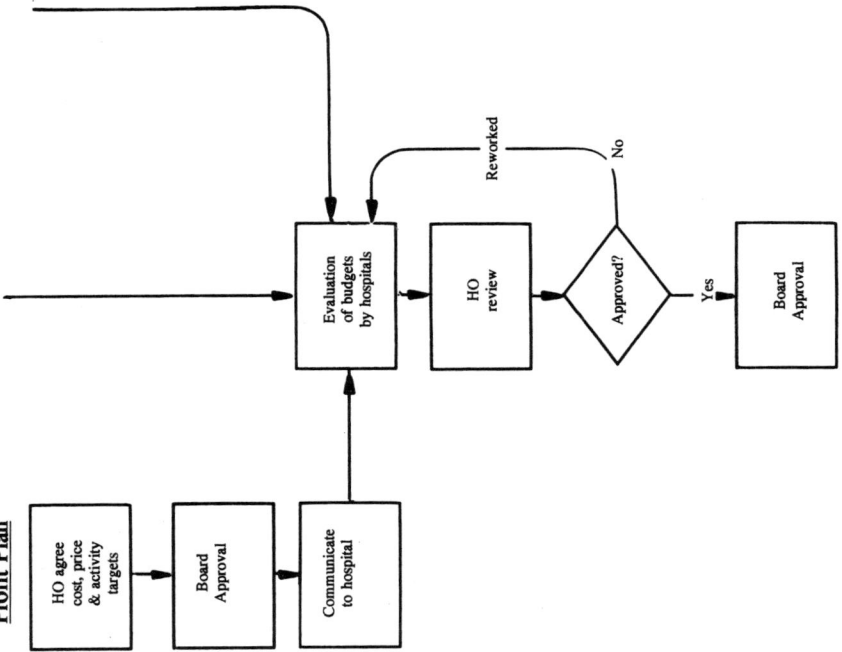

```
┌──────────────┐     ┌──────────────┐     ┌──────────────┐
│   HO agree   │     │              │     │              │
│ cost, price  │ ──→ │    Board     │ ──→ │ Communicate  │
│  & activity  │     │   Approval   │     │  to hospital │
│   targets    │     │              │     │              │
└──────────────┘     └──────────────┘     └──────────────┘
                                                  │
                                                  ↓
┌──────────────┐     ┌──────────────┐         ◇ Approved? ◇
│ Evaluation   │ ──→ │      HO      │ ──→                    ── Yes ──→ ┌──────────┐
│ of budgets   │     │    review    │         No                       │  Board   │
│ by hospitals │     └──────────────┘    Reworked                      │ Approval │
└──────────────┘                                                       └──────────┘
```

47

You should therefore split the period into months or weeks and forecast the figures for each of these shorter periods. This is particularly important when the trade has seasonal trends. Shops don't sell many Christmas cards in February!

Summary

So to summarise, the steps involved in preparing the budget are as follows:

1. Decide the period that should be covered by the budget — say one year. Also decide what periods the budget is to be divided into — for example 12 monthly periods.

2. Forecast activity levels and the income from trading and other sources for each of the periods. Remember, in many trades income does not accrue evenly over the year. Your forecast should reflect this.

3. Having established the level of sales for each month you must now forecast the cost of sales.

4. Next forecast the level of each of the overhead expenses.

5. Finally, confirm that your plan fits into your cash budget.

All through this process you should consider the links mentioned above and revise the figures as necessary.

We will go through these steps in more detail in chapters 5 and 6.

Having worked out the figures you can produce a monthly budgeted profit and loss account like the one shown in figure 9. You will note that as well as showing the budgeted figures (or forecast figures) the statement also has provision to insert the *actual* values as the year progresses. This is important because if the budget is to be a useful tool you must check to ensure that your business is actually performing as forecast. If there are significant variations then:

- You must consider why the business is not performing as forecast — where you are going wrong (or right!).

- You may need to revise your budget for the rest of the year and this may itself lead to other management decisions — will you need more (or less) staff, will you need an extra van to deal with the upturn in trade?

The Monthly Budgeted Profit & Loss Account

Details	January		February		Etc.
	Budget	Actual	Budget	Actual	
Sales					
DIRECT COSTS Purchase of Goods					
Productive Wages					
Stock Change					
Cost of Goods Sold					
Gross Profit					
OVERHEADS Motor Expenses					
Repairs & Renewals					
Telephone Charges					
Printing & Stationery					
Heating & Lighting					
Insurance					
Rates					
Bank Charges & Interest					
Professional Fees					
Sundry Expenses					
Depreciation					
NET PROFIT					

Fig. 9. Monthly budgeted profit & loss account.

As we will see in chapter 8 this review procedure must also be extended to the cashflow forecast and as a result the financing requirements of the business may be modified.

TEN TIPS FOR SUCCESSFUL FORECASTING

- The quality of a forecast depends on the quality of the assumptions made — don't skimp on the preparation work for your budget.

- Rubbish in equals rubbish out!

- Major trends only happen gradually — don't try to change the world overnight.

- Cash is the key — business activity absolutely depends on it.

- Surplus cash can lead to overconfidence.

- The future has its roots in the past.

- The activities of one period reflect and modify the next period.

- Never overlook the unexpected. As far as reasonably practical take steps to minimise disruption caused by such an event.

- If the results are not as expected then treat them with suspicion — you have probably got the model of your business wrong.

- You won't get your forecast exactly right. Play with the figures and see the effect of variations. You will find out a lot about your business this way and also how it would react to change.

CASE STUDIES: THE GARAGE REPAIRMEN

Jim and David were made redundant and each received a £31,000 redundancy payment. They each decided that they wanted to set up their own small garage workshop repairing cars.

Jim prepared a detailed budget and a cashflow forecast which he used to set his chargeout rate for his work. He worked out that (provided that he was not too extravagant setting up the business) he would be able to draw an adequate sum from the business whilst building up his reputation and goodwill.

David, on the other hand, thought that the money that he had would be more than adequate and he did not bother to make any detailed financial plans. He thought that by buying lavish equipment he would be able to undertake work quicker and cheaper than his competitors but he had not prepared a costing.

Six months later, David found that he was running out of cash. Although he had obtained work, the setting up of the business had taken longer than he had expected. Also — although he did not know it — his cut price was leading him to make a loss on nearly every job he undertook. The following month, under pressure from creditors, he had to declare himself bankrupt.

Jim's business had also started slowly, but he had anticipated this and so he had sufficient cash to see him through the period. After six months he still had adequate cash resources: because he had prepared his costings to establish the rate that he should charge to customers, he was trading profitably. Jim hopes to get some better equipment for his business next year when he has saved enough from his profits.

SUMMARY

- A budget is a financial forecast of what is going to happen as well as being the plan to steer the business.

- The budget is made up of many interlinking sections which influence each other.

- The **cash budget** is all important and can over-ride all other departmental budgets.

- Care should be used when setting the forecast.

- Even when the budget is complete you should continually monitor the business to ensure that it is still on course to achieve its target (more detail in chapter 8).

5
Budgeting for
Income and Costs

Over the next two chapters we will consider budgets in more detail. The format of a budget will broadly follow the profit and loss account, although it will also include some items of a capital nature. In preparing the budget forecast we will need to go into more detail than when drawing up the historical profit and loss account.

TYPES OF COSTS

Fixed & variable costs
It will also be necessary to appreciate that some expenses are **fixed costs** of the business and some are **variable**. Note also that some items are directly related to the production of the product of the business, the **direct costs**, whilst others are concerned with the overall running of the business and these are the **indirect costs**.

Mostly the direct costs are variable with the level of activity, whilst the indirect costs (mostly overheads) are fixed. Figure 10 shows some of the expenses of each type.

	Fixed Costs	*Variable Costs*
Direct Costs	–	Materials Freight Charges Energy
Indirect Costs	Rent Insurance Office Administration	Selling Expenses

Fig. 10. Fixed and variable costs.

Looking at the fixed and variable costs in a little more detail, we can soon appreciate that raw materials used for making into the product being sold by the business will be variable costs. The higher the level of activity, the more sales and the more purchases. Energy for production will also be a variable cost (although see below concerning semi-variable costs) as will freight charges.

But the rent that you have to pay for your factory will *not* vary with the level of sales. It will remain fixed. So too will the cost of the administrative staff salaries, the insurance on the equipment and most of the other overhead expenses. Admittedly there can be times when the level of activity will sooner or later affect these expenses. If turnover has a big increase you may outgrow your factory and need larger premises. However, generally you can regard these types of expense as fixed costs.

Semi-variable costs
Some costs at first sight appear to be variable in nature, but they cannot be regarded as truly variable. Examples might be productive labour or the provision of machines. In each case although their use to the business will vary directly with the level of activity it is not practical to have fractions of people or machines.

When the production reaches a certain limit it is necessary to take on another *whole* person or to buy another *whole* machine with all the inherent costs.

This causes a stepped effect as shown in figure 11 and it should be taken into account when we prepare the costings.

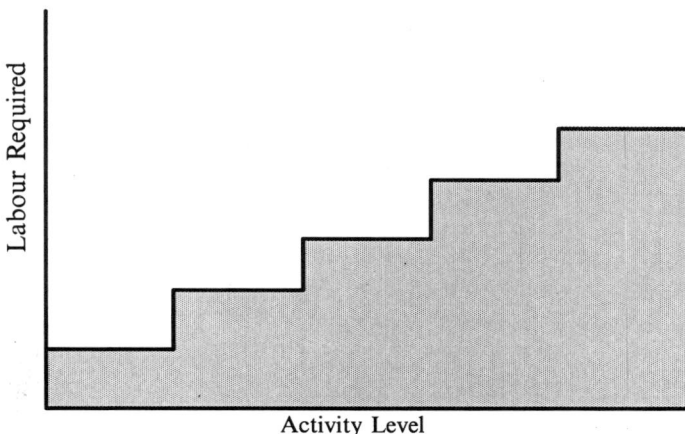

Fig. 11. Labour requirements at varying activity levels .

Selling expenses
Although these expenses are not *directly* linked to the level of activity they will follow (or even precede) the trading trends. The selling expenses are dealt with in more detail in the next chapter, but clearly the size of the sales force will be influenced by the level of sales being achieved by the business. If great interest is shown in your products you will need a suitably sized team to turn the enquiries into orders. Remember your sales team members are often the first point of contact for your potential new customers and those customers will judge your business on the way in which their enquiry is handled.

In this chapter we will deal with the creation of the budgeted gross profit. In the next chapter we will deal with overheads and capital budgets.

So where do we start?

BUDGETING YOUR SALES INCOME

The top line
The top line on the profit and loss account is generally the sales income, whether it comes from the sales of a product or from the sales of services. Although it is not the only restricting factor, very often it is the sales figure that leads the budget and everything else is fitted round it. If you are using a machine to make your product and it is already working at full capacity then this may restrict sales unless you can supplement this production capacity by some other means. For the time being we shall assume you can make all that you can sell.

So how much can I sell?
If you have been trading for some time then past experience can often be a great help in estimating present and future sales. However, care should be exercised if you are only looking at *values*. You must also consider the *number* of items sold.

Example
Consider the following. You have been consistently selling a product over the past three years at the rate of £25,000. However, over this period inflation has been running at 8% per annum. The picture in terms of unit sales would therefore be:

Sales	Value	Units
Year 1	£25,000	5000
Year 2	£25,000	4630
Year 3	£25,000	4287

A loss of unit sales has been disguised by increases in price. If the loss of sales continues but there is no further inflation to increase prices there will be a reduction in sales revenue in year 4 to £23,150. It is therefore most important to consider sales in unit values as well as monetary values.

What unit values should I use?

This will depend upon the nature of the business. For example a milkman would normally consider the gallonage of milk sold. If you are a manufacturer of ladies' dresses then you will probably use a unit of a dozen dresses as your basic unit.

What about service businesses?

For service businesses — plumbers, gardeners, architects etc each job is different, but one thing is common to all jobs: time.

For these businesses the unit of time is normally used as the basis for charging the customer and it can also be used as the basis for working out the budget. In some service businesses, for example carpet fitting, the charge is based per sq. ft. or per sq. metre. In these types of trade it is still time that is really being sold but past experience has meant the fitter now knows how long it will take him to lay a given area of carpet. He has therefore converted time into a unit that is easier for him to measure and calculate.

How else can I gauge the level of sales?

Well one thing is clear, no customers = no business. So you should find out the following:

- who your customers are

- what goods or services they want to buy

- what quality they are looking for

- what price they are willing to pay.

And to establish the information, why not ask them? Most people are happy to help you, particularly if they think that by doing so they will, in the future, be able to get the product they want. You can do this research in different ways depending upon the types of product or service you are trying to sell. If you are to open a shop selling to the public then you probably need to stand in the high street and stop some people passing by and ask their opinion. You might also do some 'door knocking' to establish local needs, likes and dislikes. Do be careful with the latter, though. Tell the police what you are doing beforehand, and if possible leave a business card with householders to put them at ease. It will also act as an advertisement.

If you are selling to businesses it may be more appropriate to write to them and follow up with a phone call. You should ask not only your existing customers but also those businesses which you have targeted as being right for your business to sell to. For example if you are marketing car components you could contact garages and car accessory shops listed in *Yellow Pages* for your geographical area.

A letter might be something like this:

Dear x

As you may be aware we are the premier distributor of Widgets in this area.

To help us to assess the needs of our customers we are carrying out a brief survey. We would value your opinion on our products in relation to your business and will telephone you during the next few days.

The survey will not take long but your views will help us to ensure that we are able to supply the exact needs of your business.

Yours sincerely

The survey itself should include questions on:

- Meeting delivery targets, price, credit period, friendly service, working hours, after sales service.

- Can you name any other suppliers of widgets (this will give you a clue about the competition).

- What most dissatisfies you about the service that we provide?

- Do you have a large demand for widgets?
  (The follow up question could then get a more specific figure.)

- Did you know that we make four different grades of widgets? In deciding which to buy can you please rate the following on a scale of 1 to 10:

  Price of product   _____
  Quality of product   _____

From questions like these you will gain a lot of valuable information about your customers' requirements. Aside from its main purpose it will also help promote your products.

From the survey you can hopefully start to get some idea of the volume of sales that you can expect, for example in a week, a month, or a year.

Factors affecting your sales assessment
You should have gained knowledge of the following matters which will enable their influence on sales to be assessed:

- The price that your targeted customers expect to pay, ie their perception of the value of the goods or service.

- The effect that changes in price will have on demand.

- Whether demand is local or national.

- The direction that the market is moving in. For example, is demand for one product reducing whilst another (possibly newer) is taking its place?

- The popularity of each item in your range of products.

- Seasonal trends (if applicable).

Armed with the above information from your market research and possibly your past experience of the business you should now be able to produce a reasonably accurate forecast of the sales of units of each of your products.

WHO SHOULD DO THE SALES FORECAST?

If you are a 'one man band' then the answer is *you*. If your business is large enough to have a sales department or administrator you may be able to delegate part of the task to them. It will depend upon the structure of the organisation and the capability of the staff concerned. Remember also that your involvement in at least part of the market research exercise will give *you* a valuable insight into the way your customers and potential customers regard your business. In addition it will give you a superb marketing opportunity to sell more products if the review is correctly handled.

Putting the budget together

Suppose that from your research you have established that there are no seasonal trends and you predict that your sales of widgets each month will be as follows:

Product type	Unit sales per month
Type A	700
Type B	1000
Type C	1500
Type D	800

You will also have established from your survey the expected selling prices of the products which are perhaps as follows:

Product type	Price each
Type A	£3.25
Type B	£4.40
Type C	£5.30
Type D	£6.90

We will consider in a moment whether these are the right prices to charge but assuming that they are accepted the monthly sales budget for widgets would be:

Product type	Units	Price	Value
Type A	700	£3.25	£2,275
Type B	1000	£4.40	£4,400
Type C	1500	£5.30	£7,950
Type D	800	£6.90	£5,520
			£20,145

If the business also makes product types x, y, z, then the sales of all of these lines of products can be combined into the overall sales budget thus:

Product line	Value
Widgets	£20,145
Type X	£17,940
Type Y	£25,695
Type Z	£18,530
	£82,310

Remember also that if your business has seasonal trends then you will need to produce separate figures for each month. You cannot just multiply the monthly figures by 12 to arrive at your forecast sales for the year.

PRICES BUDGETING

What should the selling price be?
From your research you will have established the price that your customers expect to pay and also details of your competition. You may also have been able to obtain price lists from competitive businesses to see how much they charge.

However, most of the time, you must sell your products at a profit and you therefore need to establish how much the product has cost. Occasionally you may sell a particular product at cost or even below cost as a 'loss leader'. This means that you hope sales of this product will encourage customers to buy other products from you which *are* profitable.

Separating direct and indirect costs
In establishing the cost of producing an item it is important to realise that there are two types of cost: **direct costs** and **indirect costs**. Direct costs are those incurred directly in producing the particular item or carrying out the service.

They will include materials, wages and other direct production costs such as energy.

Indirect costs are the other costs which do not relate directly to production. They include the cost of selling the product (eg advertising) and expenses such as rent, rates and insurance. Most of the indirect costs will continue regardless of the level of activity of the business.

Direct & Indirect Costs

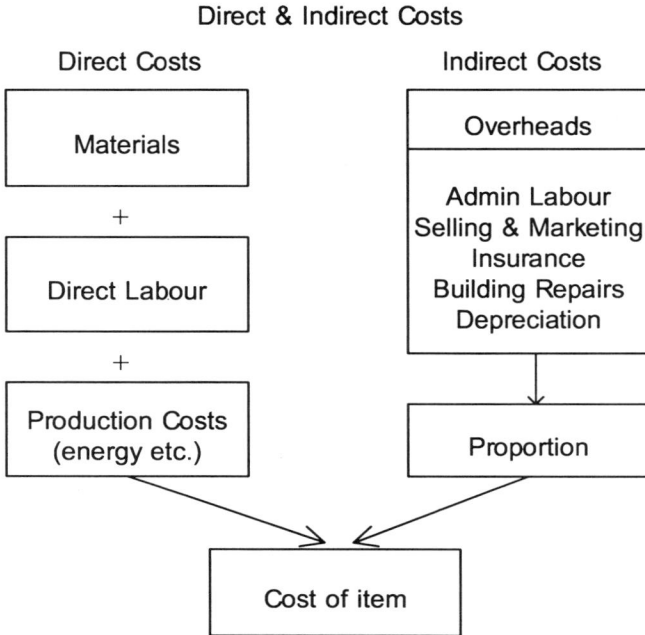

Fig. 12. Direct and indirect costs.

Example

Let us consider a product and see how each of these elements is made up. If we consider a pencil sharpener there are three components that have to be made and assembled: the body of the sharpener, the blade and the screw to retain the blade.

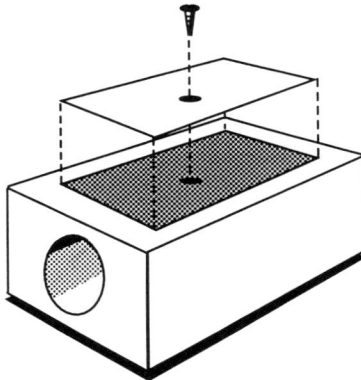

Fig. 13. A pencil sharpener.

The process is as follows:

- The body of the sharpener is cut from a piece of alloy extrusion.

- It is then drilled for the hole to insert the pencil.

- A second hole added for the screw.

- A recess is milled into the top to accept the blade.

- The blade is stamped out from a strip of steel and the hole for the screw stamped through it.

- The cutting edge is ground onto the blade.

- The item is assembled.

It is assumed that the screw has been bought in from a screw manufacturer but if this was made 'in house' then you would need to add those processes as well.

To work out the cost of production you need to consider each of these items and you will draw up a cost sheet like the one in figure 14.

You can see that it is divided into three sections.

- Materials
- Direct labour
- Production overheads.

The first two should present little problem. For materials it is a measure of the material used, with an allowance for wastage, priced out at its cost to the business. For the labour it is the time taken to complete each process charged at the appropriate rate per hour.

However the third element of the costing may require a few words of explanation. Production overheads include the cost of:

- Supervisor's wages
- Maintenance wages
- Tools and consumables
- Repairs to machines
- Energy (electricity, gas, oil)
- Rent, rates
- Depreciation of machines etc.

COST SHEET

Product: Alloy Pencil Sharpener
Standard Quantity: 1000
Drawing:P693

Materials

Part No.	Specification	Std Qty	Waste	Qty Req'd	Price/Unit	Value
A472	Alloy Extrusion	11 mts	8%	11.88 mts	16p/mtr	£1.90
S142	Steel Strip	25 mts	5%	26.25 mts	7p/mtr	£1.84
S078	Retaining Screw	1000	2%	1020	£1.78/1000	£1.82
						£5.56

Labour

Operation No	Operation	Std Hrs	Rate/Hr	Value
Body A1	Guillotine - Alloy	0.15	£4.75	0.71
2	Drill - Pencil Hole	0.45	£5.25	2.36
3	Drill - Screw Hole	0.35	£5.25	1.84
4	Milling	0.28	£5.42	1.52
Blade B1	Stamping of Blade from strip	0.07	£4.75	0.33
2	Grinding	0.15	£5.25	0.79
Assembly C1	Assembly	0.83	£4.50	3.74
				11.29

Overheads

Operation No.	Operation	Std Rate	Value
A1	Guillotine	200% DL	1.42
2	Drill	180% DL	4.25
3	Drill	180% DL	3.31
4	Milling	325% DL	4.94
B1	Stamping	300% DL	0.99
2	Grinding	275% DL	2.17
C1	Assembly	£2.75 per Hr.	1.88
			18.96
	Total works cost per standard quantity		35.81
	Cost each		3.581p

DL = Direct Labour

Fig. 14. A cost sheet.

The costs of all of these items are assessed. Where they can be directly related to a production operation then this is applied. Where this is not possible, for example selling expenses, then the costs should be apportioned to the production departments on an appropriate basis for example in ratio of direct labour hours or on the basis of the cost of direct labour.

As mentioned earlier, many of the overhead costs continue regardless of the level of activity, and so you need to be able to forecast the level of activity to apportion the overheads on an accurate basis (see the table on page 41 concerning the apportionment of overheads at different levels of activity).

Returning to the example in figure 14 you will see that the cost of producing the pencil sharpener is 3.581p.

If from our research we have established that the market will be prepared to pay 4.25p per item then we will earn 0.669p profit per item (15.74% of sales).

However if we find that we can only obtain 3.25p per item then some hard decisions must be made. The costings will need to be re-examined to see if there is any place where additional savings can be made. If for example the market is sufficiently large and buoyant then introducing longer working hours on a two or three shift system may possibly be one answer. Many of the overhead costs will be fixed and therefore a doubling or trebling of production does not lead to a doubling or trebling of overheads. The overhead cost is therefore apportioned between a larger number of items bringing about a reduction in the value per item.

Break-even analysis

One technique that you can employ here is called **break-even analysis**. You will recall that expenses of a business can be segregated into **fixed costs** and **variable costs**. Fixed costs are incurred by the business according to time and will include all the overhead costs such as rent and insurance whilst variable costs are incurred for the production of the product itself. The total costs of running the business are therefore the sum of the fixed costs and the variable costs incurred during the period. The more items you produce then the higher the **total cost** but even if you produce no items you will still have to pay for the fixed costs. This is illustrated graphically in figure 15(a).

In the example the fixed costs are £500 per week and the variable

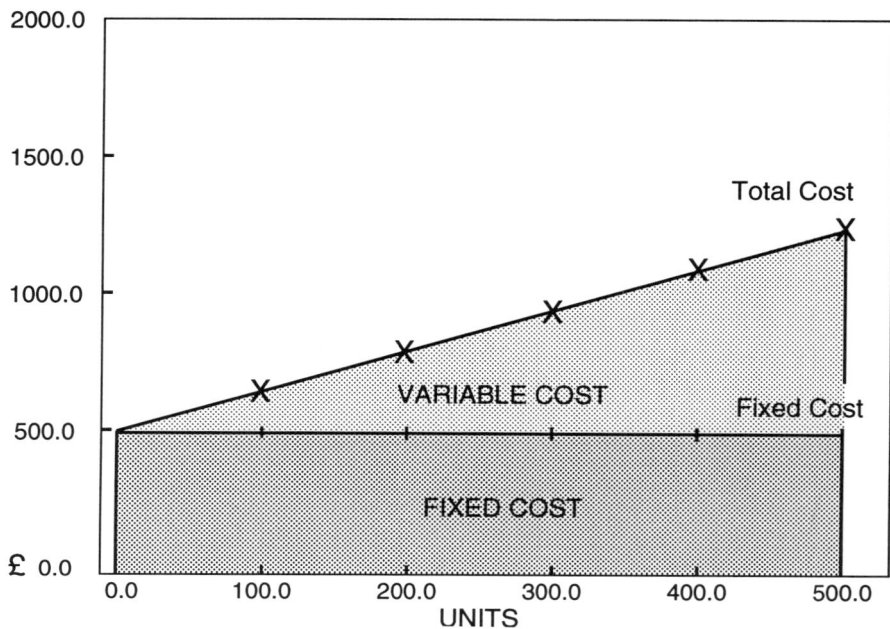
Fig. 15 (a). Cost of production at varying activity levels.

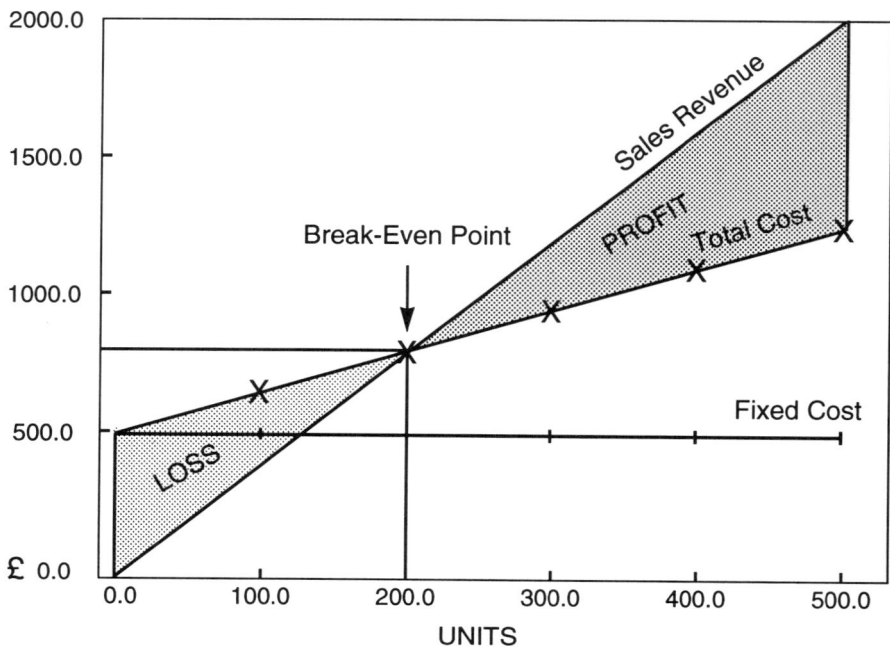
Fig. 15 (b). Break-even point.

Fixed and Variable Costs
Break-even Calculations

Unit numbers		0	100	200	300	400	500
Fixed Costs per week –	£500	500	500	500	500	500	500
Variable Cost per Unit –	£1.50	0	150	300	450	600	750
Total Cost		500	650	800	950	1100	1250
Sales per unit – £4		-	400	800	1200	1600	2000
Profit/Loss		-500	-250	0	250	500	750

Figure 15 (c). Break-even calculation.

cost is £1.50 per item. If you refer to the table at figure 15(c) you will see that the total cost rises from £500 per week if no units are produced to £1,250 if 500 are produced.

If we add a further line on the graph (as shown by figure 15(b), we can also trace the **sales revenue**. If the selling price is £4.00 per unit then the sales revenue rises from zero at no sales per week, to £2,000 at 500 sales per week. At a level of 200 sales the sales revenue line crosses the total cost line. This is the **break-even point** — the point at which the business makes neither a profit nor a loss.

So how do I calculate the break even point?

Whenever you sell an item, part of the proceeds are used to meet the variable costs – the costs of making that specific item. The rest is applied towards the payment of the fixed costs and hopefully the profit. This remainder is referred to as the **contribution** from the sale of the product.

Thus if the product sells for	£4.00
And the variable costs are	£1.50
The contribution is therefore	£2.50

This means that for every item sold you receive £2.50 towards the fixed costs of the business. Going on from here, if the fixed costs are £500 per week then if you have sold 200 items you will have received (200 x £2.50) £500 of contribution from the sales and broken even. If you sell less items you will make a loss: if you sell more then you will make a profit.

The break-even level can therefore be calculated by dividing the fixed costs by the contribution per item, thus:

$$£500 \div £2.50 = 200$$

Using this technique you can assess what level of production and sales you need to make a profit (or at least not make a loss).

You may however be able to produce the item for much less than the selling price expected by your customers. In this case you may consider reducing the selling price to try to grab a larger share of the market.

But a note of caution. If you reduce your price then sales have to make a huge increase to maintain the same overall profit. This would be revealed by the break-even analysis above but consider the following:

If you are currently earning 15% gross profit then:

% price reduction	% increase in sales volume
0	0
-2.0%	+15%
-3.0%	+25%
-4.0%	+36%
-5.0%	+50%
-7.5%	+100%
-10.0%	+200%

Unless this is fully appreciated then it is *very dangerous* for a business to reduce its prices. Businesses cut prices believing that they will maintain profit because of the increased volume of turnover and fail to realise the enormous effect on profit that such action will cause. When the profits fail to materialise they cut prices still further to boost turnover – the result, business failure!

A full table setting out the effect of pricing policy against sales volume is included at appendix 3.

If as a result of reviewing costs you decide to adjust the prices then you will need to rework the sales forecast as set out on page 58. You can now also work out the cost of these sales and produce a direct cost forecast as follows:

Direct Cost Budget

Widgets	Unit	Price (£)	Value (£)
Type A	700	2.75	1925
Type B	1000	3.75	3750
Type C	1500	4.50	6750
Type D	800	5.90	4720
			17145

The gross profit from widgets is therefore forecast to be:

	£
Sales	20145
Costs of production	17145
Gross profit	3000

In the next chapter we will see how the gross profit fits into the overall budget arrangement.

SUMMARY

- Expenses can be divided into **fixed** and **variable** costs.

- Fixed costs do not vary with activity levels.

- Variable costs increase with higher levels of activity.

- You should choose a unit of production, such as *barrels* of beer or *reams* of paper as your basic cost unit and all your costs should be related to that unit.

- For service businesses the unit of production is time.

- Carry out market research surveys to establish the expected level of sales so that you can forecast your income.

- Cost out the expense of producing the product. This may involve drawing up a **cost sheet** incorporating each of the individual processes necessary in arriving at the finished product.

- Prepare **break-even** calculations to ensure that the forecast sales will cover the overheads.

- Don't be tempted to cut the price of your product in the hope of winning extra sales — you will have to make a *very* large increase in sales just to earn the same profit.

6
Budgeting for
Overheads and Capital Items

In the last chapter we discussed how to forecast the level of sales, the direct cost of the products sold, and how to calculate the gross profit expected from the trading.

In this chapter we will look at the other expenses of the business. Although primarily we will concern ourselves with *revenue* expenditure we will also look at the *capital* budget.

BUDGETING FOR OVERHEADS

If you look at figure 12 on page 60 (direct/indirect costs) you will see that in considering the cost of an item we have so far concentrated on the **direct costs** on the left of the diagram. We now need to consider the **indirect costs**.

Fortunately in some ways most of these costs are fixed in nature which makes it easier to prepare the budget.

Overheads include the following:

- stationery
- clerical wages
- management and supervisory salaries
- cleaners' and caretakers' wages
- rent and rates
- telephone and fax
- travelling
- motor expenses
- insurance
- bank charges
- entertaining
- depreciation
- accountancy, audit and legal fees

Let's consider these in turn:

Stationery

This item covers the cost of general stationery requirements of the business. It will to some extent vary with the level of activity. Remember that it includes:

- letterheadings
- invoices to customers
- copier paper
- statement forms
- pens, pencils, typewriter ribbons, laser printer cartridges etc.

If you are preparing a stationery budget for an existing business you can base it on actual expenditure in previous periods, allowing for known factors such as price increases and changes in the level of business activity. If you are preparing the budget for a *new* business, try to assess the likely quantity that you will use of each type and price the items either from stationery catalogues or by asking your local printer (you will need to give him an order anyway).

Clerical wages

Once again for the *established* business you can assess clerical wages by adjusting the wages for the previous period by known factors. For a *new* business you need to assess how many clerical staff you will need (list their duties, to help you understand it fully) and then price their cost by looking at rates quoted in job advertisements. Remember that you may also have to add employment costs for some items such as Employer's National Insurance.

Management and supervisory salaries

The comments above concerning clerical wages also apply here.

Cleaners' and caretakers' wages

The comments above concerning clerical wages again apply here.

Rent and rates

Rent

If you are using rented property then the rent charged by the landlord should already be known.

Rates

Non-Domestic Rates (ie business rates) are based at a rate in the pound on the rateable value. The rate of non-domestic rates is set each year. For 1996/97 the rate was 44.9p in the £. Rateable values of business properties were reviewed in April 1990 and again in April 1995. In broad terms the rateable value should roughly equate to the amount of rent payable for the property.

Telephone and fax
There are two elements to these charges:

Rental
The line rental (and if applicable the equipment rental) can be easily established. Contact your local BT sales office free by dialling 152.

Calls
This is a little more tricky. It will depend on how you run your business and only you can assess this. If you make a lot of long distance calls then this can be a sizeable amount. Ask BT for the tariff (see number above) and try to estimate the number and duration of your calls. Remember, a fax can often work out cheaper than a phone call.

Postage
Once again the budgeted amount will depend on the nature of your business. If you have a lot of heavy catalogues to despatch then this could prove a considerable item. Otherwise, for general correspondence and invoices etc just include a token amount.

Travel
This is another cost that will vary widely from one business to another. Some businesses require very little travel; others require the payment of rail fares and hotel accommodation nearly every day. You know your business and should be able to estimate accordingly.

Motor expenses
Like travelling expenses this item is something that will depend very much on the way you run your business. Estimate according to your own circumstances.

Insurance
There are several types of insurance that a business is likely to need. These include:

- public liability
- employer's liability
- building insurance
- equipment insurance
- consequential loss insurance
- product insurance.

If you are already in business you will have a good idea of the costs of these various insurances. If you are just starting your business then you should certainly consider the insurance aspects — there is too much at stake to overlook this topic. Contact a professional insurance broker. Not only will he or she be able to advise you on what insurance you need but also the cost — so that you can include the figures in your budget.

Bank charges
Most banks have published a tariff of charges. This is a good starting point but remember that the basis of charges is negotiable (although less so than it was a few years ago); a chat with your bank manager may prove worthwhile.

Entertaining
Just like travel, this item will very much depend upon the nature of the business and how it is run.

Depreciation
This reflects the loss in value of equipment, motor vehicles and other fixed assets over the years. Although this is a **revenue** expense we will consider it in more detail whilst talking about **capital budgets** later in this chapter.

Accountancy, audit and professional fees
The charges from your accountant will depend upon a number of factors:

- The state of your bookkeeping.

- The services you ask him to undertake (is he to calculate the wages and VAT?).

- Choosing the right accountant. Generally the smaller firm with say two partners will be able to provide an economic and yet reliable service for the smaller business. To engage one of the large national firms for this work would be taking a sledge hammer to crack a nut — and the fees will reflect this. Ask your accountant for a quotation for dealing with your work.

Other professional fees are less regular in nature. It may be necessary to consider a charge for debt collection or for other services that are special to your particular business.

Advertising and marketing

When you established the sales budget this was achieved, at least in part, by conducting a customer survey. This should also have given some indication as to the need for advertising and marketing. Will you need to have brochures printed? — ask a printer for costs. What advertising will you need? Apart from a 'splash' advert when a new product is launched it is often best to limit the size of adverts. Of course you want to keep your name in the public eye, but it is the case that little and often produces better value for money than a large advert placed infrequently. Remember, too, that you need to *target* your advertising. If you are a manufacturer of car accessories, then advertise in *Motor* or *Autocar*. If you make computers then advertise in *Personal Computer World* or *What Computer*. In this way you will get your message across to those who want to buy from your business without wasting money and effort on those who don't.

Summary

Each of the above overheads must be considered in turn and the relevant figures built into the overheads budget, an example of which is shown at figure 16.

Selling & distribution expenses

There is a further class of overheads that you should also consider. This relates to the cost of selling and distributing your products. It can be subdivided into four sections, each of which can be further subdivided as follows:

Sales representatives
- salaries
- commissions
- travel and motor.

Administration Budget
12 months to 31 March 19XX

	Previous year's Actual £	Current Budget £
MATERIALS: Stationery Sundries SALARIES & WAGES: Management Clerical Cleaners & Caretakers Sundries EXPENSES: Rent & Rates Telephone Postage Travelling Entertaining Insurance Bank Charges Audit & Accountancy Fees Subscriptions Depreciation Sundries		
	£	£

Fig. 16. Administration overhead budget.

Sales office
- salaries
- communications (telephone, fax, postage)
- office supplies (stationery etc)
- accommodation (rent, rates, heat and light)

Publicity
- salaries

- advertising
- samples
- sundry costs (stationery and general office costs).

Warehousing, packing and despatch
- salaries and wages (supervisors, packers and drivers)
- warehouse costs (rent, rates, heat and light)
- packing materials
- vehicle costs
- carriage charges.

You can now draw up the selling and distribution budget like the one shown in figure 17.

Finally each of the summary budgets (including the sales and direct cost budgets discussed in chapter 5) are combined together in the overall **revenue budget** an example of which is shown at figure 18.

BUDGETING FOR CAPITAL ITEMS

Although it is vital to forecast the revenue budget, the importance of the capital budget must not be overlooked. Whereas the revenue budget has dealt with the day to day running costs and income of the business, the **capital budget** deals with the provision of new machines, extensions to the factory, replacement of motor vans etc. The capital expenditure has only a limited effect on the profitability of the business, but as will be seen in the next chapter it has important consequences for cashflow.

How capital expenditure affects profits
The amount of capital expenditure may affect the profitability of the business in two ways.

- By increasing the **depreciation** charge — you will recall that depreciation reflects the loss in value of the fixed assets during the period and clearly the more that you have invested in this area the more that there is to lose.

- It is likely that investment in new equipment or buildings will involve some form of finance which will in turn have an **interest charge** of some sort. Even if you do not need to borrow money to carry out the project it still has a cost in that it is reducing the amount that would otherwise be available for you to invest. There is therefore a loss of investment income.

Selling & distribution budget
12 months to 31 March 19XX

		Previous Year's Actual £	Current Budget £
REPRESENTATIVES: Salaries Commissions Entertaining Travel Costs			
	Total	£	£
SALES OFFICE: Salaries Office Supplies Postage Telephone Rent & Rates			
	Total	£	£
ADVERTISING & PUBLICITY: Salaries Office Costs Advertising Catalogues Samples Sundries	Total	£	£
WAREHOUSING, PACKING & DESPATCH: Supervisors' Salaries Packing Wages Drivers' Wages Vehicle Costs Sundries			
	Total	£	£
	Grand Total		

Fig. 17. Selling and distribution budget.

How capital expenditure affects cashflow

The timing of capital expenditure may have significant effects on the cashflow of the business. Although new machinery and equipment must be available to meet increased sales demands it is important not to incur the expenditure too early and bear the financing costs before the increased revenue from the extra sales arrives. As will be seen in the next chapter this is therefore a balancing act. Initially you should forecast your capital expenditure budget to record not only *what* additional equipment is needed but also *when* it will be needed to meet the forecast sales demand. Remember that some items require quite a long **lead time**: an extension to the factory cannot be built overnight. You must work out when it is required and then make an allowance for its building or installation.

Overall Revenue Budget
12 months to 31 March 19XX

| | Products | | | Total £ |
	Type A	Type B	Type C	
Sales				
Cost of Sales				
Contribution to Profit	£	£	£	£
Selling & Distribution Overheads				£
Administrative Overheads				£
Total Overheads				£
Budgeted Profit				£

Fig. 18. The revenue budget.

SUMMARY

• Quantify the amount of each type of overhead expense. For example, work out the expected cost of stationery used by the business during the year.

• From the above forecasts, prepare the overheads budget.

• Assess the costs of selling and distribution, and prepare the budget to cover these costs.

• These forecasts of gross profit (see chapter 5) and overheads, and selling and distribution costs can be combined to form the overall revenue budget.

• Do not forget the capital budget. Although it will have little effect on the profitability of the business the *timing* of the purchase of assets is of prime importance when considering cashflow (see chapter 7).

7
Managing Cashflows

INTRODUCTION TO CASHFLOWS

The cashflow forecast runs hand in hand with the budgeted profit and loss account.

- The profit and loss account takes account of transactions at the time that the expense *accrues* to the business and the income is earned.

- The cashflow forecast deals with the transactions at the *time of payment*. For example, if goods are sold on credit it may be a month or two before payment is received. Equally, when you purchase goods you may be able to take 30 days to pay for them.

Although these items will be recorded in the profit and loss account for the month that the goods arrive (or are despatched) there will be a delay before the transactions have any effect on the bank account. In the same way some overhead expenses will be paid on an irregular basis instead of evenly over the months. For example insurance is normally paid for twelve months in advance whilst the benefit of having the policy accrues evenly throughout the year. These differences in timing must be incorporated into the cashflow statement.

The cashflow forecast must also take account of capital expenditure for equipment or plant for use in the business.

Cash is the lifeblood
Cash is the lifeblood of a business — it makes the wheels of business go round and for the reasons stated above cash does not necessarily flow at the same time as sales. One of the main reasons for business

failures is having insufficient cash available to meet liabilities as they fall due. Having prepared a budgeted profit and loss account, it is essential to review the cash situation of the business to ensure the finance will be there to make the whole thing possible. To liken this to Philip's budget in the first chapter, if his mum had said that his uncle was to give him £5.00 he might recognise that he was to receive some income but he could not spend the money until it was actually received.

If cash is the life blood of the business, then sales are the heart that pumps it back to the beginning of the system. This is illustrated at figure 19. The **total funds** available to the business are used for the **purchase of materials** and the payment of **labour costs**. Some funds are also used to purchase machinery which in turn earns its place in the business by helping to make the product. These elements all combine to make the product, and through **sales** this produces the cash to make the cycle flow again.

VAT

It is also important to consider the effect of VAT on the cashflow. This is discussed in more detail later in this chapter.

PREPARING A CASHFLOW FORECAST

The important thing to remember about the cashflow statement is that it is dealing with movement of **cash**. Here we mean cash in its widest form, including transactions passing through the bank but *not* transactions involving items purchased or sold on credit. Why is this so important?

Example

Well, consider the following. You sell goods on credit in January but the customer takes 60 days' credit before making payment. The money from the sale is therefore not received until March. So although you have made the sale and earned your money, how do you pay the wages at the end of January or February? This is why the banks place so much emphasis on cashflow and often insist that their customers produce cashflow statements to them; otherwise they know that they will be expected to provide the necessary bridging finance. However you must keep in mind that you may also sell goods in February which are paid for in April and goods sold in March will be paid for in May and so on. So in fact it is not *temporary* finance that is needed but *long term* finance. Therefore, in

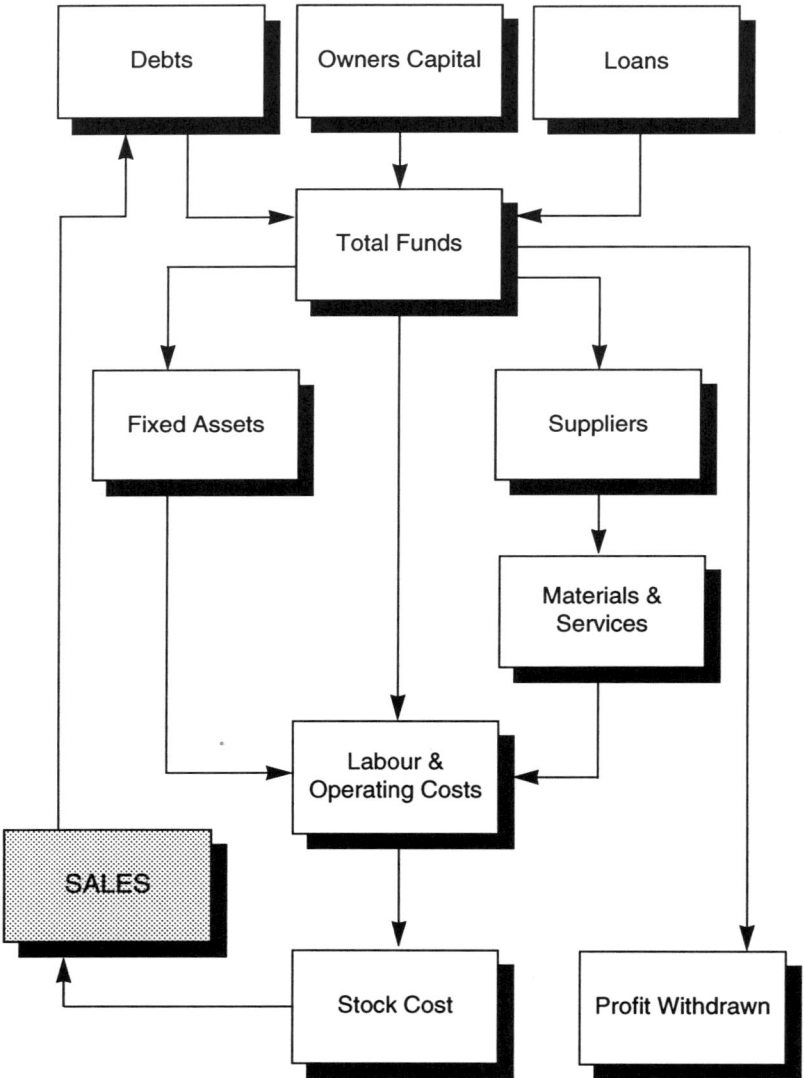

How Cash flows through a business

Debts	Owners Capital	Loans

Total Funds

Fixed Assets

Suppliers

Materials & Services

Labour & Operating Costs

SALES

Stock Cost

Profit Withdrawn

'Sales' is the pump that keeps the system working

Fig. 19. The cashflow system.

drawing up the cashflow statement we must consider the *timing* of payments and receipts.

As mentioned above the banks consider the preparation of a cashflow statement of prime importance, and rightly so. To assist their customers most produce standard forms like the one in figure 20 to help make the process simpler.

The first thing to decide is the period of the forecast. This might be three months, six months or a year. Periods longer than a year are likely to be unreliable: a year is a long time in business.

You should also decide how many periods you are going to break the forecast into. On a short forecast covering, say, three months you may decide that you should use weekly periods. A short forecast like this can be prepared with a lot of detail and a reasonable degree of accuracy. A forecast looking forward for six or twelve months and divided into monthly periods is more normal and should give a good general indication of the cashflow trend of the business.

Longer forecasts are possible. Sometimes it is decided to produce a **five year plan**. In this case the periods chosen will probably be calendar quarters and although it can be used to show general trends it is unlikely to prove very accurate at the end.

Using a printed cashflow forecast form
Looking at the form in figure 20 you will see that it is divided into the following sections:

A. Dates of the periods.

B. Opening balance (initial balance or F from previous month).

C. Income.

D. Expenditure.

E. Increase or Decrease in Cash (C-D).

F. Closing balance (B +/- E).

Note
The closing balance of one month becomes the opening balance for the following month.

The headings
Within the sections for income and expenditure are some standard headings but blank lines are also provided so you can add your own

✖ The Royal Bank
of Scotland plc

Name of Company, Firm etc _____

How to complete the Form

1 Insert the date in the month when your cash position is likely to be at its lowest (A).

2 Enter the Opening Bank Balance on that date in (B). This is the balance at the Bank — not in the Company's/Firm's etc books. Receipts paid in but not credited to the Bank Account or Cheques Issued, but not debited to the Bank Account should be included in the Income/Expenditure column.

3 Income/Expenditure includes all items which pass through the Bank Account. Enter each item in the column under the date by which it is expected to be debited/credited. (Note likely variations, Bank Holiday short weeks etc).

Enter the dates chosen (A)													
Opening Bank Balance Credit/Debit (B)													
	Projected	Actual	Projected	Actual	Projected	Actual	Projected	Actual	Projected	Actual	Projected		
Income													
Cash Sales													
Debtors													
Other Income (please specify)													
Total Income (C)													
Expenditure													
Cash Purchases													
Creditors													
Wages and Salaries													
PAYE													
Heat, Light and Power													
Rent													
Rates													
Bank Charges (quarterly)													
Interest Charges (quarterly)													
Hire Purchase Payments													
Loan Repayments													
VAT (Payments)													
Tax													
Dividends													
Other Expenditure (please specify)													
Total Expenditure (D)													
Cash Increase/Decrease (E)													
Closing Bank Balance Credit/Debit (F)													
Actual Bank Balance in question													
Variation from Forecast Favourable/Adverse													

0186Q/3/85·

Fig. 20. The cashflow forecast.

For the period from _____ to _____

4 The difference between Total Income (C) and Total Expenditure (D), representing the net cash flow for the period, should be entered on line (E), in the column for the relevant date, as an increase or (decrease) whichever is applicable.

5 As a final step, the amount of the difference (E) between Total Income and Total Expenditure should be added to, or subtracted from, the Opening Bank Balance (B) to arrive at the figure representing the Closing Bank Balance to be inserted on line (F) in the appropriate date column. The Closing Bank Balance (F) at the end of any given period should be carried forward as the Opening Bank Balance (B) for the subsequent period.

															Total	
Actual	Projected	Actual	Projected	Actual	Projected	Actual	Projected	Actual	Projected	Actual	Projected	Actual	Projected	Actual	Projected	Actual

details as necessary. Note also that some expense items that you correctly included on the budgeted profit and loss account should not be included on the cashflow statement because they are *not* transactions involving the movement of cash. Principally these are depreciation of plant, equipment and motor vehicles. Although there will be a diminution in the value of these fixed assets through time, no cash is paid out to reflect this. Since the cashflow statement only involves *cash* transactions depreciation should be ignored for the purpose of this statement.

Let us now look at the breakdown of income and expenditure in more detail.

FORECASTING CASH INCOME

Income has been divided into the following:

- Cash sales
- Debtors
- Other income.

Forecasting cash sales

Cash sales are sales made where payment for the goods is received immediately. For example, if you run a shop most of your sales will be cash sales; you will not have to wait before you receive payment. As mentioned earlier, when preparing a cashflow forecast *cash* is meant in its widest form. For the shopkeeper cash sales will include all sales where immediate payment is received.

So it will include:

- cash
- cheques
- Access or Visa payments (from the retailer's viewpoint these are credited to the bank account in the same manner as a cheque receipt).

You will need to work out the cash sales in each period. If you have prepared a detailed monthly budget then this can easily be transcribed. If not then you will now have to work out *when* the sales will take place. Remember seasonal trends and build these into your cashflow model: ice cream sales high in July and August — sales of Christmas crackers high in December, etc.

Enter the figures for each week or month into the 'Projected' column on the form. We will look at the column headed 'Actual' in the next chapter.

Forecasting debtors

Remember that on the cashflow forecast we are looking at the *cash transactions*. We do not need to record when the *sale* is made. What is important is the date we expect to receive payment. Returning to the example at the beginning of this chapter, although we sold goods in January it is March — when the proceeds are received — that we need to fill in on the form. Assuming that we are using monthly periods then January's sales will be entered on the form in the March column, February sales in the April column, and March sales in the May column etc.

As with cash sales you can transfer the figures from your detailed budget if available, making due allowance for the period of credit (see below). If you have not prepared a detailed budget then you will have to work out the figures now. Look at the earlier chapters on budgeting for guidance on how to forecast the level of sales; remember to allow for seasonal trends.

You must also decide how much credit your customers are likely to take. Bear in mind that if you offer customers 30 days' credit they will no doubt sneak a few extra days. It is likely to be 45 or even 60 days before you actually receive payment. It is most important to keep on top of your debtors. You can easily tie up a lot of uncollected cash in debtors, increasing your financing costs and perhaps being hassled by an irate bank manager complaining that your overdraft is too high. Also remember that you can't pay the

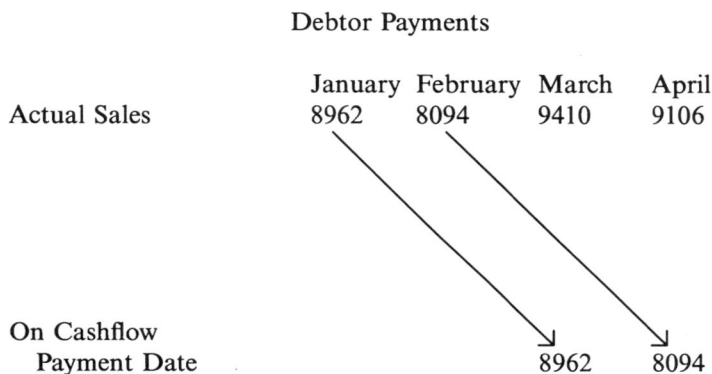

Debtor Payments

	January	February	March	April
Actual Sales	8962	8094	9410	9106
On Cashflow Payment Date			8962	8094

Fig. 21. Debtor payments.

bills with debtors — you need *cash.*

Never underestimate the period of credit taken by your customers: err on the conservative side and assume that they are *all* going to take those extra days credit.

When you have estimated how much credit will be taken you can work out when you will receive payment. You can then enter the credit sales proceeds figure into the appropriate column on the form.

Forecasting other income

This is a 'mopping-up' heading. The entries made will depend upon your business. If for example you expect to receive refunds of VAT (eg farmers often have VAT refunds) then these cash receipts can be recorded here. We will consider VAT in more detail later in this chapter because it is most important that it is treated correctly.

Other items which may be included within this section are:

- money put into the business by the owner
- loans received by the business
- rent received.

Include the appropriate figures in the column corresponding to the month when you think that the cash will be received.

FORECASTING CASH EXPENDITURE

Just as the income section was divided into different classes, so is the expenditure section. Let's look at some of these in turn.

Cash purchases

These are payments for goods or materials for the business where no period of credit is taken. For the shopkeeper this might represent goods that he purchases from the Cash-and-Carry for resale. You will need to give similar consideration to the matters raised when looking at cash sales above.

Creditors

Your creditors are those that you owe money to and in this context it is the payments to the creditors that need to be considered. When we looked at the **debtors** and credit sales above we discussed the period of credit that would be taken by your customers. In looking at **creditors** you are looking at the other end of the transaction: how much credit can *you* take from *your* suppliers? If credit is offered (provided you do not fool yourself and forget that you will need to pay for the goods at some time) then you may as well make use of the period of credit. That period of credit represents *free finance* for your business. If you borrow the money from the bank to pay the bills you will have to pay interest but suppliers' credit comes at no charge. How much extra credit you can squeeze out of your suppliers is up to you. If you overdo it they will refuse to supply you which could put you in a difficult position and unable to make your product.

Wages and salaries

There is little that needs to be said here. There may be some seasonal trends to allow for, and you may need to build into your model an adjustment for a pay review but in general these expenses accrue fairly evenly each week or month throughout the year.

PAYE

The amount of PAYE you will have to pay depends on the level of wages and salaries, and its calculation is beyond the scope of this book. It is made up of two elements, one of them further divided as follows:

- Income Tax

- National Insurance
  employee's contributions
  employer's contributions

Once again it is the *timing* of the payment that is important, and that depends upon the value. If the *monthly* value of PAYE due to the Collector of Taxes is less than £450.00 then you can account for the money to the Inland Revenue on a quarterly basis as follows:

Quarter to	*Pay by*
5th July	19th July
5th October	19th October
5th January	19th January
5th April	19th April

In this case the payments should be included on the cashflow forecast in July, October, January and April. If you do not qualify for the quarterly payments then you must pay the PAYE to 5th of each month by 19th of that month.

In simple terms this means that one month's PAYE should appear in the following month on the cashflow.

Heat, light and power

The main expenses to be included under this heading are gas and electricity although it could also include heating oil or coal. The point to make is that the payments are not made monthly (unless you are a large consumer or on a budget scheme) and so you should include the payments in the months that they will fall due. For gas and electricity this will normally be each quarter and you should slot in the figures in the appropriate columns. Remember, there are often marked seasonal trends and fuel consumption is higher during the winter quarters. Coal and oil purchases must also be included in the correct columns when you estimate what you will pay for these services.

Rent

Rent is normally due quarterly on the following 'usual quarter days':

- 25th March
- 24th June
- 29th September
- 25th December

Include the quarterly rent payments in the appropriate columns on the form. If the rent is payable monthly or even weekly then include the normal rent payments in each of the columns across the form.

Rates

Rates are normally payable by two instalments each year. The exact timing for the payments varies from one local authority to the next. Check your rates account to see the exact dates of payment and include the figures in your cashflow forecast accordingly.

Some businesses pay their rates by monthly instalments throughout the year. If you use this scheme include the monthly payment in all the columns across the form.

Bank charges

The amount your bank charges will depend, at least in part, on the way you run your business and manage your account. It costs the bank money to operate and in turn this cost will be passed on to you.

Some of the bank's services are more expensive than others. For example the handling of coins and notes (particularly coins) is a costly business. If you regularly pay coins into your account, or draw change from the bank, then you will be charged for the privilege.

Sometimes you can avoid these charges by coming to arrangements with other local traders. The supermarket which needs lots of change can make an arrangement with the local milkman and take his change in exchange for notes. This way both benefit, because both are saved bank charges related to the handling of coins.

If you do not know the basis of the charges on your account then ask at your local branch. Most banks now have printed tariffs. In this way you can reduce your bank charges by making simple changes to your banking routine. It will also give you a clear insight into the cost of running your bank account so that you can include the relevant figures in the cashflow forecast. Bank charges are usually levied on a quarterly basis in March, June, September and December. Include the relevant figure in the appropriate columns on your cashflow form.

Interest charges

Interest charges are the sums levied for borrowing money, generally a percentage of the sum borrowed. The main lender will probably be the bank for the business but money can also come from private loans or from other financial institutions.

Although interest on money from loans would come within this general description it is perhaps better dealt with under the heading **loan repayments** (see below). This section mainly deals with the interest charged on bank overdrafts.

As mentioned above interest charges are generally a percentage of the sum borrowed. The rate of interest charged is often related to **bank base rate** which can be found from the national newspapers. Bank base rate is the measure of the value of money to which most interest rates are related. Borrowers have to pay a **premium** (extra amount) over base rate (normally between 2% and 6%) and investors are paid a little less than base rate. The difference between the rate paid to the bank by borrowers and the amount paid by the bank to investors is their 'turn' on the money. This is how the banks earn their profit on the service.

The rate of interest that you are charged 'over base rate' is mainly influenced by how much risk the bank sees in its lending to you. If there is a low risk then there will be a small margin over base rate, the higher the risk the higher the margin.

Your bank will tell you what rate you are being charged on your overdraft. You must then calculate the interest charge represented by this level of borrowing. Like bank charges, interest charges are normally levied on the account (by direct debit) on a quarterly basis in March, June, September and December. To calculate the figure:

Step-by-step
(a) Work out the average overdraft balance for the quarter by:

    i. Adding together the 'Opening Balance' figures (shown at 'B' on the form) for the three month period. Eg add together the figures for April, May and June. Ignore any months where the balance is in credit: the bank is unlikely to pay you any interest on any credit balance, but if they do it is likely to be at such an insignificant rate that it can be ignored for this purpose.

    ii. Divide the total by the number of items that you added together, that is the number of months overdrawn in the quarter. If you have been overdrawn throughout the quarter this will be 3. This will give you the average overdrawn balance.

(b) Add your margin over base rate to the current bank base rate to establish the actual rate of interest that *you* will be charged.

(c) Calculate the value of the interest charged by:

    i. Multiplying the average balance by the interest rate *and*

    ii. Dividing by 100 to arrive at the annual interest charge, *then*

    iii. Dividing the above result by 4 to establish the charge for the quarter.

Example
Overdrawn bank balance

April	5942
May	4763
June	6651

Bank base rate	7.5%
Margin over base rate	3.5%

Step (a)
i.	$5942 + 4763 + 6651 = 17356$
ii	$17356 \div 3 = 5785$

Step (b)   7.5 + 3.5 = 11

Step (c)
   i.   5785 x 11 = 63635
   ii   63635 ÷ 100 = 636
   iii   636 ÷ 4 = 159

Thus the interest charges for the quarter would be £159.

Enter the interest charges so calculated into the appropriate columns relating to the quarterly payments on the cashflow statement.

You will see that every time you alter one of the figures on your cashflow it will alter the value that you should include for an interest charge. For this reason the bank interest charge should be one of the last figures that you put in — but don't forget it!

Hire purchase payments and loan repayments

For the purpose of the cashflow forecast these can be taken together. They are treated similarly.

Capital and interest

The repayments that you make for these expenses consist of two elements.

- The **capital** element — the repayment of the original loan or the payment for the cost of the goods.

- The **interest** or finance element — the charge made for providing the money.

When we were considering the budgeted profit and loss account we were only interested in the *interest* element of this charge: only the interest element affects the amount of profit earned by the business. However, when we are looking at cashflow we must consider *both* aspects of the payment — the capital elements must be paid out of cash just like the finance costs.

Normally both hire purchase and loan repayments are made at a fixed monthly rate. This figure should be included in the monthly columns on the cashflow forecast.

If you are considering a new project it may be worth referring to the repayment table at appendix 1 to help you work out the monthly repayment.

VAT payments

VAT payments are normally due to the Customs & Excise each quarter but the exact date of payment will depend upon your own VAT registration. As VAT influences all aspects of business we will deal with it separately in more detail at the end of this chapter.

Tax

Calculating tax liability is beyond the scope of this book. However, we can touch briefly on the dates of payment of tax. The timing of taxation payments will depend upon the status of your business.

Types of business
This will be in one of two categories:

- A **limited company**. The tax will be due nine months after your company year ends.

- A **sole trader** or **partnership**. The tax will be payable in two instalments due on 1st January and 1st July.

You should incorporate the appropriate sums in the relevant months on the cashflow.

Dividends

Dividends are only relevant to companies. They are payments made to those who own shares in the company. In small companies the timing of dividend payments is normally set to benefit cashflow. The amounts of the dividend will depend upon the profitability of the business.

Other expenditure

Like the heading 'Other Income' this is a mopping-up heading. It includes items such as:

- capital expenditure on plant equipment
- drawings taken out by the proprietor or by a partner.

BUILDING VAT INTO YOUR CASHFLOW

As you have seen in chapter 3, VAT applies to most transactions in business. If you are registered for VAT purposes you will need to build it into your cashflow. Just how you do this will depend upon whether you are on a **cash accounting basis** or the **invoice basis** because this will affect the *timing* of the VAT payment.

If you are not registered for VAT then the value of the VAT charged to you just becomes part of the goods.

When we prepared the budgeted profit and loss account we excluded VAT from all the transactions. We only looked at the underlying value of the goods. In preparing the cashflow, however, we must remember that the business must pay the VAT over and along with the purchase price when the goods are purchased. Equally it will receive payment of VAT when its customers pay for the goods or services supplied.

There are therefore two aspects to consider when preparing the cashflow forecast.

- the VAT paid to suppliers or received from customers
- the payments (or refunds) of VAT to the Customs & Excise.

Overall the VAT transactions will balance off: the **output** that you receive from your customers on your sales will be paid to the Customs & Excise Department; the VAT charged to you on purchases (**input**) will be claimed as a credit from the VAT office. However, *timing* of the transactions and the value involved means that it cannot be ignored. On many occasions, businesses which have not made adequate provision to pay their VAT liability have run into financial difficulty.

Accounting for VAT on an invoice basis

If you account for VAT on the **invoice basis** then it is the time that the goods are *invoiced* that must be considered when preparing the cashflow statement.

Output tax on sales

As you will recall from chapter 3 VAT is normally dealt with on the quarterly VAT return and is payable by the end of the month following your VAT quarter. So, if your VAT quarter runs from 1st January to 31st March, you must account to the Customs & Excise for the VAT by 30th April.

When preparing the cashflow statement you must include the VAT output tax on all sales that you made during the quarter, regardless as to whether you have been paid for the goods or not.

Input tax on purchases
In the same way as the output tax, you can obtain credit for all goods purchased and invoiced to you during the VAT quarter. You can then set this figure of input tax against the output tax; using the above example it would only be the *net* figure that you must pay to (or request refund from) the Customs & Excise in April.

Accounting for VAT on the cash accounting basis
If on the other hand you are using the **cash accounting basis** for VAT then it is the *time of payments* that matters when accounting for VAT. Suppose your goods are sold in February but you do not receive payment until April; then, assuming that your VAT quarters are the same as the calendar quarters, you must pay over the VAT to the Customs & Excise in July. Had you been on the **invoice basis** then the payment to the Customs & Excise would have been in April. Likewise credit for the VAT on purchasers can only be taken at the time the goods are paid for.

So how do I incorporate VAT into my cashflow?
As discussed above, the timing of the VAT transactions differs according to the VAT accounting scheme adopted by the business.

It is often better to prepare a separate document on which to work out the VAT (see figure 22). The VAT calculation will break down into 3 elements:

- output VAT

- input VAT

- accounting for VAT to the Customs & Excise.

When you calculated the budgeted profit and loss account, you did so excluding VAT. As you have seen above we must now incorporate VAT into the cashflow forecast. One way to do this would be to add the value of the VAT onto each of the items of sales or purchases which is subject to VAT. *But there is an easier way* if you are using the cash accounting scheme.

On cash accounting
On your VAT schedule you record the VAT-exclusive value of the transactions subject to VAT in the *month of payment*. Then you can work out the VAT due on the total sales or purchases. You will notice that on the schedule at figure 22 no reference is made to items such as

```
Schedule of VAT Calculation
                        Jan      Feb      Mar      Apl      May     June     July     Aug

OUTPUT TAX

Sales                  8962     8094     9410     9106     9880     9562

Other Items Subject
   to VAT                -        -        -        -        -        -
                    -----------------------------------------------------------------
                       8962     8094     9410     9106     9880     9562
                    =================================================================
VAT @ 17.5% - Outputs  1568     1416     1646     1593     1729     1673
                    =================================================================
                                                                                    Etc.
INPUT TAX

Cash Purchases          268      242      282      273      296      286
Creditors              2688     2428     2823     2731     2964     2868
Heat, Light & Power     313      283      329      318     ·345      334
Rent                   1200                        1200
Other                   868     1316      304      774      318      152



                    ------------------------------------------------------------
                       5337     4269     3738     5296     3923     3640
                    ============================================================
VAT @ 17.5%             933      747      654      926      686      637
                    ============================================================
Net VAT Due             635      669      992      667     1043     1036
                    ============================================================
Qty Payment to Customs & Excise                   2296
                                               =========
```

Fig. 22. VAT calculations (for incorporation within the cashflow forecast).

wages or rates. This is because there is no VAT charged on these expenses. However although VAT output tax will mainly occur on your sales, it can also be affected by other transactions. If for example you dispose of a piece of machinery or a van that you have used in the business then you must also account for VAT on these sales.

The total of the **outputs** (items on which output VAT is charged) and the total of the **inputs** is then established and the VAT calculated at the standard rate.

Are part of your sales standard rated and part zero rated? If so, you will have to estimate the value of each type of sale and only include the standard rated sales on the schedule. Likewise if part of your purchases are zero rated then the element must be excluded from the figures on your VAT schedule.

On the main cashflow statement these amounts of VAT are recorded in the 'Other income' and 'Other expenditure' sections as 'VAT received on sales' and 'VAT paid on purchases' respectively.

Back on the VAT schedule, it is easy to calculate the net VAT position for each month by deducting the Input VAT figure from the Output VAT figure. The quarterly payment to the Customs & Excise is then found by adding together the 3 months of the VAT quarter. Remember, you have until the end of the month following the VAT quarter to sort out your VAT so the payment (or receipt) will appear in the month following the end of the quarter. If your VAT quarter ends on 31st March the payment to the VAT office will appear in April.

On invoice basis for VAT

If you are using the invoice basis for accounting for VAT then matters are slightly more complicated; the recording of the transaction for VAT purposes and the time of payment may be different. On this basis it is easiest to gross up the items from the budget profit and loss account so that they appear on the cashflow statement inclusive of VAT. To do this, multiply each item subject to VAT by 1.175 to arrive at the gross figure.

You will however still need to prepare a VAT schedule in order to work out the amounts of VAT due to (or from) the Customs & Excise. The form of the Schedule will be the same as that used under the cash accounting basis (see figure 22). But this time, instead of recording the transactions at the time that payment takes place you should record them at the time that they are invoiced.

FITTING IT ALL TOGETHER

Near the beginning of the chapter we said that the cashflow forecast was divided into six sections thus:

A. dates of the periods
B. opening balance (initial balance or F from previous month)
C. income
D. expenditure
E. increase or decrease in cash (C-D)
F. closing balance ($B +/- E$).

By now you should have entered the period date in section A and all the figures in sections C and D. The initial bank balance should be entered in the first column of section B. Then it's pocket calculator time!

Add the items to arrive at the totals for income and expenditure each month (sections C and D). Deduct the total expenditure from the income to arrive at the increase or decrease in cash. Write this in section E. Note that it is easier to show negative figures in (brackets) so that they stand out. Add or subtract this figure to or from the opening balance, to calculate the forecast bank balance at the end of the first month (item F).

This now becomes the opening balance for the second month, and your calculation begins again.

When you have finished, the closing balance line across the bottom of the schedule shows the predicted finance required for the business. You will see where your overdraft peaks. You will then know if the budget that you have drawn up is feasible or whether your cash requirements are too great.

If you cannot finance the budget then it's 'back to the drawing board!' You will have to start again and see how you can adjust your budget and your business plan to arrive at figures that you can manage.

This may involve planning for a slower growth of the business so that the working capital required can be financed from profits. Or it may mean postponing building an extension to the factory, because although it would make life easier you could manage without it until the business gets a little bigger. There are all sorts of adjustments that you could make but do not be tempted to 'fudge' the figures to arrive at the answer you want. This way you will only be fooling yourself and time will find you out.

Drawing up the budget and cashflow in this manner is a relatively painless way of finding out if your plan will work. If it fails at this stage what have you lost? — a few hours, a few sheets of paper and some ink.

If you had gone ahead and the plan had then failed you might have lost your business, your home and your whole way of life.

Case study – Mark in a muddle

Mark had prepared a cashflow forecast for his business using one of the standard forms given him by his bank. According to his forecast his overdraft was going to show a rapid reduction. The bank manager had seemed sceptical but pleased when the figures had been produced to him.

Some months later Mark discussed the figures with a friend. The expected drop in the overdraft did not seem to be happening. They discussed the figures at some length and eventually it transpired that when Mark had prepared his cashflow statement he had become confused between cash sales, sales, and money from debtors. He had assumed that cash sales meant the invoices sent out to customers each month and had included all his sales invoices. He had correctly deduced that 'cash from debtors' referred to the cash received from his credit account customers.

Both figures had been included in the forecast and so he had duplicated the value of his credit sales. It was not surprising that he was finding it difficult to live up to the planned forecast!

This true example illustrates the need to look at the figures that you are preparing with great care. When things do not appear quite right, make sure you fully understand the reason why. The cashflow statement *only* deals with the movement of cash — not sales on credit until the cash is actually received. If you are unable to resolve your doubts about your figures then you should ask for help from your accountant.

Summary

- Cash is the life blood of a business — without it the business will die.

- Timing of actual cash payments or receipts is the critical factor in preparing the cashflow forecast.

- Banks consider the preparation of cashflow statements to be of prime importance — they produce standard forms to help.

- Remember that some expenses such as insurance or rent may not be payable evenly throughout the year — you must include the expense in the month in which it will actually be paid.

- Don't overlook bank interest.

- VAT can have quite an influence on the cashflow — make the appropriate adjustments.

- If things don't look right on your forecast, ask the reason why!

8
Monitoring Performance

So far we have seen how to prepare the forecast profit and loss account and balance sheet and also the projected cashflow statement. However no one can forecast matters completely accurately. If they could they would win the football pools every week and wouldn't need to be in business at all!

You will therefore need to compare what you have forecast against what is actually happening and then act accordingly. As an analogy, if you live two miles to the west of a town and want to drive there to do some shopping, you forecast that you must drive east. But if you drove with your eyes closed you would very soon end up in a hedge or hit another vehicle. Of course what really happens is that you start off in your forecast direction, east, but you look where you are going and what is happening and keep modifying your course so that you stay on the right road.

So it should be in business. You start on the forecast course but you need to modify your actions in the light of what is really happening.

MONITORING YOUR CASHFLOW FORECAST

If you refer back to the cashflow statement at figure 20 on page 82, you will see that as well as columns for *projected* figures there are also columns headed *actual*. At the end of each month you should complete the appropriate column with the income you actually received from cash sales and debtors etc, and the expenditure you actually paid out on each category of expense. The maths is then the same as before when you prepared the forecast. You can then compare how each item has performed against the forecast. You can also note the difference between the *forecast* closing bank balance and the *actual* balance at the bank.

There will always be some differences. If the difference is substantial you should investigate why. If the difference is in your favour you need not worry, but you should still find out the reason. After all by building on the successful elements of the business you should be able to strengthen it further.

On the other hand if the business is not living up to expectations it is really crucial to establish where the problem lies. This may be that the business is not performing in accordance with the budget or it may be timing differences which are causing problems with cashflow.

Example
Let's assume that:
– widgets sell for   £5.00
– widgets cost   £2.80

– you allow your customers 30 days' credit.
– you plan to take 30 days' credit from your suppliers.

– general overheads are £1,800 per month.

When the cashflow goes according to plan
Your planned sales are:

Budget	Jan	Feb	Mar	Apr	May
Units	1000	1200	1250	1350	1500
	£	£	£	£	£
Sales value	5000	6000	6250	6750	7500
Purchases	2800	3360	3500	3780	4200
Overheads	1800	1800	1800	1800	1800
	4600	5160	5300	5580	6000
Profit	400	840	950	1170	1500

Your planned cashflow should therefore be:

Cashflow	Jan	Feb	Mar	Apr	May
INCOME					
Sales	-	5000	6000	6250	6750
EXPENDITURE					
Purchases	–	2800	3360	3500	3780
Overheads	1800	1800	1800	1800	1800
	1800	4600	5160	5300	5580
Surplus/ Deficit	(1800)	400	840	950	1170
Opening Balance	-	(1800)	(1400)	(560)	390
Closing Balance	(1800)	(1400)	(560)	390	1560

When the cashflow forecast does NOT go according to plan

What happens if instead of taking one month's credit your customers take three months before they pay you?

Cashflow	Jan	Feb	Mar	Apr	May
INCOME					
Sales	-	-	-	5000	6000
EXPENDITURE					
Purchases	-	2800	3360	3500	3780
Overheads	1800	1800	1800	1800	1800
	1800	4600	5160	5300	5580
Surplus/ Deficit	(1800)	(4600)	(5160)	(300)	420
Opening Balance	-	(1800)	(6400)	(11560)	(11860)
Closing Balance	(1800)	(6400)	(11560)	(11860)	(11440)

In this case all the sales were made as forecast but your customers took longer to pay than you expected. So instead of having an overdraft of just £1,800 in January, repaid in April, you had one of just under £12,000, assuming that the bank would allow it. Only in May does it start to be repaid.

CHASING DEBTORS FOR PAYMENT

So how do I 'keep tabs' on my debtors so that I can chase them?

First let's clear one thing up. **Debtors** are those that owe you money: you owe money to your **creditors**. Some people confuse the two terms.

So it's your **debtors** that you will have to chase for payment. It's all very well saying to yourself, 'oh — they will pay sooner or later'. That way it is more likely to be later, and remember that the longer that a debt is outstanding the more likely it is to turn into a bad debt. The other aspect to consider is whether you can afford to allow the credit period? The example above shows how soon you can run into financial problems if you let things slide.

All businesses that sell goods or services on credit must have some system for keeping track of who has paid and how much is outstanding. This can either be by way of a full **ledger** system (keeping a separate account for each customer) or some simpler system.

The simplest way to keep track of who owes you money is to have two files for your sales invoices — one for the unpaid invoices and one for the paid invoices. When someone pays you find the copy of the invoice in the unpaid file, write the date of payment on it, and transfer it to the paid file. The invoices that are left in the unpaid file are for the people that owe you money — the ones to chase.

Having got a system to identify who owes you what you should prepare a monthly summary listing the amounts. Add up the amounts due from each customer and make a list of the sums outstanding. If when this is prepared you 'age' the debts this will give you a good indication of which customers to chase for payment. You should do as shown on page 104.

This is known as an **aged debtors list** (sometimes referred to as a **debtor matrix**). From this it is easy to see who owes you money and how long it has been outstanding. In the example you will see that S Harvey is a very bad payer — the debt has been outstanding for over 90 days. J Palmer also owes money from between two and

Aged Debtors

Name	Total	0 – 30 days	30–60 days	60 – 90 days	Over 90 days
M Deacon	210	210			
C Hammond	490		490		
S Harvey	980				980
K & J Milner	520	520			
J Palmer	1255	583		672	
P Whitaker	375	375			
	3830	1688	490	672	980

three months ago. These two definitely need chasing for payment and C Hammond should also receive a reminder to say that the money is overdue.

Note also that J Palmer obtained some more goods last month. If a customer consistently pays late, ask yourself whether you really want them as a customer? They are costing you money through increased interest charges on your overdraft and also putting your business at risk by increasing the pressure on your cashflow.

Because slow payers can cause real problems for your business you should adopt an action plan for the collection of debts. Here is one set out below:

Days after invoice
- 30 days   send statements to customers
- 44 days   send letter asking for the reason for non-payment
- 51 days   send reminder letter for the previous letter
- 58 days   telephone the customer and obtain a firm commitment regarding the date for payment
- 65 days   send a notice before taking legal proceedings
- 77 days   place the debt in the hands of the court for judgement

Even if you get judgement against your customer you may still be unable to recover the debt, but you can at least be sure that you have done what you could to recover the debt.

An example of the 44 day letter is shown at figure 23.

YOUR BUSINESS CO.

279 High St
Howtotown
Northshire

A Debtor & Co   2 September 199X
13 Owing St
Dueham
Indebtedshire

Dear Sirs

Re Overdue Amount £154.97

We refer to the statement sent to you recently and we are
sorry to note that we have not yet received payment of the
amount that is now overdue.

If you have some query then please advise us. If not then
please mail your cheque today as we are sure you will
appreciate that our normal credit terms have been
exceeded.

Yours faithfully

Fig. 23. A debtor chase letter.

MONITORING YOUR BUDGETS

So far we have looked at cashflow problems caused by timing errors such as debtors taking extended periods of credit. But there could be a more fundamental cause of the problem — you got the budget wrong! The budget is of course a *forecast* of what is to happen, and just like the weather forecast it is not always correct. For this reason you will need to check that what you forecast is actually happening. I'm sure that the weather forecaster looks out of the window sometimes just to make sure that, if he forecasted rain, it *is* actually raining!

One approach is to prepare a full set of accounts every month, and in the largest of businesses this is just what happens. However for your business this is likely to be excessive. You would spend more time preparing the monthly accounts than you would actually running the business.

In practice therefore the work can be restricted. Normally the overhead expenses can be forecast with a fair degree of accuracy. In any case, they are often not the major item, so that even if there is an error in the forecast it is unlikely to throw the whole budget out of balance. The more likely area for error is in forecasting the level of sales and the direct costs.

By restricting your work to these matters you can often produce figures quite quickly and easily; they will be sufficiently accurate for you to monitor the business and see if there are any material fluctuations from the budget. To do this you should prepare an abbreviated profit and loss account like the one shown at figure 24. See how the statement concentrates on the vulnerable area of the budget — the direct costs and income. The overheads have just been included as an estimate so that a profit figure can be struck.

One item which may cause problems is stock. Often the value of stock does not vary much from one month to the next although there may be some seasonal trends and you can therefore use a reasonably accurate *guestimate*. If the stock value varies a lot, and it is a material amount that would cause the accounts to show a completely wrong figure of profit then you have two alternatives:

- Take stock each month and evaluate its costs (likely to be very time consuming!)

- Introduce a **stock control system**. You record the amount of each line of stock on a separate **stock account** in a ledger so that without physically counting the stock you can quickly evaluate its value.

Your Business Co
Profit & Loss Account

	June		YTD	
	Budget	Actual	Budget	Actual
Sales	25000	24033	75000	72209
Purchases	16750	16524	50250	48647
Stock Movement	+450	+273	+650	-212
	17200	16797	50900	48435
Wages	4500	4370	13500	13129
	21700	21167	64400	61564
Gross Profit	3300	2866	10600	10645
Overheads (estimated)	1800	1800	5400	5400
Profit	1500	1066	5200	5245

Fig. 24. Monitoring the profit and loss account.

You will also note in figure 24 that provision has been made for actual figures to be added to the budget so that a comparison can be made to check the actual performance against the budget. As well as looking at the particular month, the figures for the **year to date** (YTD) are also recorded for comparison purposes. As you go through the year, enter the actual figures in the appropriate column and review the differences that are revealed. Small differences can be safely ignored but larger differences between the budget and the actual results should be investigated.

The differences may of course be favourable rather than unfavourable — not all differences are bad news. If sales are racing ahead of the forecast then this is probably a good thing. With higher than expected sales there is a greater than anticipated contribution towards the overhead costs and as a result the business should be more profitable. However do not overlook the cashflow aspects or you may run into problems as a result. Remember that cashflow is very dependent upon the *timing* of payments and receipts; if debtors are increasing as a result of the higher sales then they will require some financing. You may be able to use 'free finance' by delaying payments to your own creditors but this tactic must be used with care. If there is a big variation from the budgeted figures then you should rework the cashflow to ensure that the necessary finance will be available or to provide you with adequate warning so that alternative arrangements can be planned.

MONITORING STOCK LEVELS

It is sometimes said that 'a lean business is a healthy business'. We have already looked at one area which can result in problems with cashflow – excessive debtors. The same is true of excessive stock. Whilst you must have sufficient stock for your needs it is only too easy to carry excessive stocks which tie up cash and do little to contribute towards profit.

So how do I know how much stock I should have?
This will depend upon a few factors:
- amount of sales of that particular product;
- delivery times;
- discount policies on purchasing;
- if the product is the raw material for a process carried out by your business then the size of the processing batch will be relevant;
- its value.

From past experience you may know that you sell about 50 of a particular item each month and so feel that you should always have some of these items on the shelves to meet customers' requirements. In this case you may say, 'I must not let the stock fall below 10 items.' However if it takes two weeks to get the goods from the date of placing the order you would normally expect to sell about 25 items during those two weeks. If you wait until you have only 10 on the shelf before placing the order then you will run out before the next batch of goods comes through. Instead you should set the order level at, say, 35 so that there are actually 10 left on the shelf when the next batch is delivered. This 10 gives a **margin for error** in case the next delivery is a day or two late or if there is a higher than average demand (see figure 25).

Go through your stock and set the reorder level so that you can always ensure that you have the stock to meet customers' demands — but without carrying too much stock. You may also review this by calculating the **stock turnover ratio** (see below).

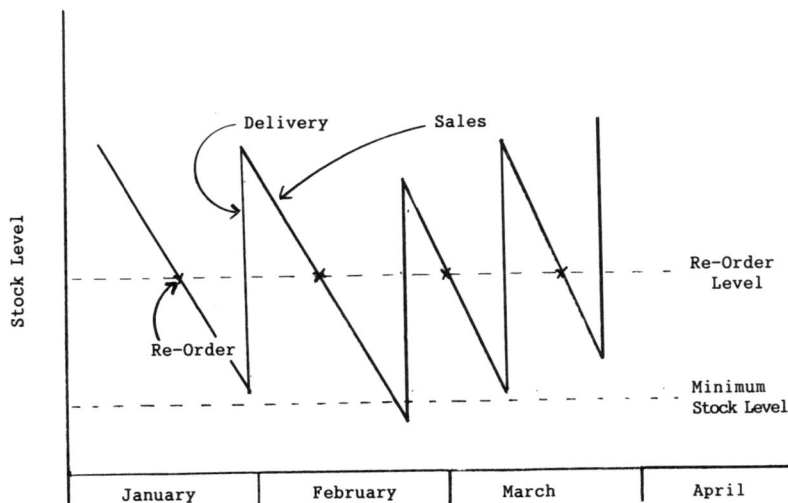

Fig. 25. Stock ordering.

USING FINANCIAL RATIOS FOR MONITORING

One of the difficulties in looking at the figures shown by your management accounts is in understanding just what they really mean to the business. This is where ratios are often useful. A ratio is merely the correlation between two numbers. For example, suppose in a street there are five houses, two with red doors and three with blue doors. The following ratios are formed:

the ratio of red doors to blue doors is 2:3
the ratio of red doors to houses is 2:5

By themselves, these figures are fairly meaningless. But in business if you compare the ratio with that in earlier periods, or against that from a business similar to your own, then it begins to become more useful. Most types of businesses have typical ratios that can be used as the benchmark against which you can measure your own business.

Four types of financial ratio
Financial ratios break down into four groups:
- **profit ratios** – they show how good the business is at making money from the capital invested.

- **efficiency ratios** – they show how good the management is at running the business.

- **liquidity ratios** – they measure the **working capital** within the business.

- **solvency ratios** – they show how near the business is to going bust.

You can learn a lot by calculating these ratios for your business. Let's consider them in turn.

Looking at the profit ratios
There are three useful ratios that show how profitable you are:

- the gross profit margin
- the net profit margin
- the return on capital

The gross profit margin
The **gross profit margin** is probably the most important ratio and
gives a good guide to ensure that your business is 'going along the
right lines'. It applies more to merchandising businesses than to
service businesses. However — depending upon the exact set-up —
it can often be applied to both types of business. The gross profit
margin calculates the relationship between the gross profit and sales
by applying the following formula:

$$\frac{\text{Gross profit} \times 100}{\text{sales}} = \text{gross profit margin}$$

The net profit margin
The **net profit margin** is similar except that it shows you the ratio
after the deduction of all expenses of the business except tax. It is a
less reliable pointer to the health of the business than the gross
profit margin but nevertheless a useful one. It is calculated as
follows:

$$\frac{\text{net profit} \times 100}{\text{sales}} = \text{net profit margin}$$

The return on capital ratio
The **return on capital ratio** measures the income being generated
from the capital invested in the business. This ratio lets you compare
the income produced by the business with income from various
other forms of investment. After all, you may earn more by having
your money invested in the building society and you can sit at home
with your feet up!
    The ratio is calculated this way:

$$\frac{\text{Profit before charging interest and tax}}{\text{total capital employed}} = \text{return on capital}$$

This ratio must be used with a little care because it can ignore one
very important aspect — the capital profit that is being made on the
assets of the business. If for example you have a freehold shop in a
prime development area, and the business is ticking along without
making any spectacular profits, then this ratio is likely to show a

poor return on capital. However the value of the premises may be going up by leaps and bounds. It is unlikely that this will show in the accounts because it is usual to show assets at their historical value rather than their current value. Without a revaluation of the assets this capital profit will be hidden until the eventual sale of the shop but it is nevertheless a very real profit when you are looking at the return on capital.

Efficiency ratios
Efficiency ratios break down into three groups, each of which further divide thus:

- **Debtors**
  Debtors turnover ratio
  Debtors collection period

- **Creditors**
  Creditors turnover ratio
  Creditors payment period

- **Stock**
  Stock turnover ratio
  Average stock holding period

These ratios show how efficiently the capital of the business is being used. For example we have already seen on page 102 just how important it is to make sure that your debtors pay you promptly. Using the ratios you can get a measure of just how efficiently your policy for collection is working.

Checking your debtor ratios
The **debtor turnover ratio** is the first of this group of ratios that we will look at. It shows the number of times that the unpaid debt is 'turned over' and is calculated like so:

$$\frac{\text{sales}\ (+\ \text{VAT})}{\text{debtors}} = \text{debtors turnover ratio}$$

Note: in order to compare like with like you will have to adjust the sales figure to include the VAT on those sales if you are registered for VAT.
     A more useful and meaningful ratio is the **debtor collection period**.

This shows the average number of days that it takes you to collect your debts:

$$\frac{\text{debtors} \times 365}{\text{sales} \, (+ \, \text{VAT})} = \text{debtor collection period (in days)}$$

This ratio will really show whether your debt collection policy is working!

Checking your creditors' ratios

In a similar manner you can also calculate the **creditors' turnover ratio** and the **creditors' payment period** with the following formulas:

$$\frac{\text{Purchases} \, (+ \, \text{VAT})}{\text{creditors}} = \text{creditors' turnover ratio}$$

and

$$\frac{\text{creditors} \times 365}{\text{Purchases} \, (+ \, \text{VAT})} = \text{creditor payment period}$$

Remember, it is important to monitor the credit period as well as the debtors. If you try to extend the period of credit too much, your suppliers may stop deliveries and withdraw your credit on future supplies. Keeping this in mind, your aim should be that the creditor period should not be less than the debtor period, otherwise you will have to finance the additional debtors and your business may then run short of cash.

Checking your stock ratios

The final batch in this group of ratios relate to stock. In the same way as the ratios have been calculated for debtors and creditors the **stock turnover ratio** and **average stock holding period** can be calculated thus:

$$\frac{\text{cost of sales}}{\text{stock at cost}} = \text{stock turnover ratio}$$

and

$$\frac{\text{stock at cost} \times 365}{\text{cost of sales}} = \text{average stock holding period}$$

Note: because you would normally value the stock at cost *excluding* VAT there is therefore no need to add the VAT to the cost of sales figure when applying these formulas assuming that you are registered for VAT purposes.

Stock lying on the shelves is not earning profit. It is important that you should hold the minimum stock that will enable you to meet the requests from your customers. This will be indicated by a high stock turnover ratio and a low average stock holding period. In these circumstances it is sometimes said that you are 'making your stock work for you'.

Liquidity ratios

The next group of ratios to look at are those measuring liquidity. We will consider the following:

- the current ratio
- the quick ratio
- security interval

The liquidity ratios show the ability of the business to meet its liabilities as they fall due from the assets that it possesses. Generally a business should have sufficient current assets to cover its current liabilities.

Checking the current ratio
The **current ratio** measures this ability like this:

$$\frac{\text{current assets}}{\text{current liabilities}} = \text{current ratio}$$

You will remember from chapter 2 that **current assets** are items such as stock, work-in-progress, debtors, cash at the bank, and cash in hand. **Current liabilities** are amounts owed by the business to its suppliers (creditors), and bank overdrafts. Current liabilities exclude items such as long term loans which do not normally fall due for repayment within twelve months.

The current ratio will usually be between 1.5 and 2. If it is less than 1, you are probably relying on a bank overdraft secured on the long term assets of the business, or delaying payments to your creditors. Either way your requirement for working capital should be an area for concern and you should ask yourself whether you are generating enough funds to meet the liabilities you are incurring.

If this ratio exceeds 2 then you may not be making the best use of your current assets. You may have too much cash in the bank, possibly not earning much interest, or too much stock or too many debtors.

Checking the quick ratio
The current ratio tests all current assets and current liabilities, but perhaps a better test is to concentrate on those assets which are cash or 'near cash'. This is where the **quick ratio** comes in. Assets such as stock and work-in-progress may be difficult to sell and convert into cash to pay the liabilities of the business and so these are excluded; only those *quick assets* that are left — cash, money at the bank and debtors — are included. The ratio is calculated like this:

$$\frac{\text{'quick assets'}}{\text{current liabilities}} = \text{quick ratio}$$

This ratio is usually between 0.7 and 1, although it does vary according to the nature of the business.

Checking the security interval
Lastly in this group we will look at the **security interval**. This measures how long the business could survive if no more cash was received but if it continued to pay its normal expenses as they fell due. It is calculated in this way:

$$\frac{\text{'quick assets'}}{\substack{\text{operating expenses} \\ \text{(expressed as a daily figure)}}} = \text{security interval}$$

As a guide this interval is typically between 30 and 90 days, although again it does depend upon the type of business.

Solvency ratios
The final group that we will examine are the solvency ratios. We will look at two ratios here:

- the solvency ratio
- gearing

Checking the solvency ratio
If your total liabilities exceed your total assets then your business is technically insolvent ('bust') and this is expressed in the **solvency ratio:**

$$\frac{\text{total assets of the business}}{\text{total liabilities of the business}} = \text{solvency ratio}$$

If this produces an answer of less than 1 then you are insolvent! You may even be committing a criminal offence to continue to allow your business to trade whilst it is insolvent so you must take care to review this figure if there is any danger of that.

Just because the ratio is greater than 1 does *not* mean that the business is alright and can immediately discharge all its debts. For example, it may have money tied up in property or equipment which is difficult to sell quickly, so that while it is not insolvent it cannot make the necessary payments as they fall due. This is why the **liquidity ratios** that we considered above are so important.

Checking the gearing
The ratio of the money that the business has borrowed (on loans, overdrafts and hire purchase etc) to the capital invested in the business by shareholders or the owners of the business (including accumulated profits if they have not been withdrawn) is referred to as the **gearing** of the business. This is calculated like this:

$$\frac{\text{total borrowed}}{\text{owners' capital}} = \text{gearing}$$

The gearing of a business is an important guide to how much the business should be allowed to borrow. In general banks expect their lending to the business to be at least matched by the investment of the owners or shareholders. This means that a ratio of less than 1 should be expected. Exceptions are occasionally made if there is a known 'track record' for the business and the cashflow and profits are steady.

By using ratios you can check on the trends for your business and also strike comparisons with similar businesses.

CASE STUDY: THE RIVAL RAINCOAT FACTORIES

Bill owned a small factory making ladies' raincoats. George operated another raincoat factory half a mile down the road. It had been a wonderful summer — which was bad news for Bill and George! Sales had slumped and were now at an all time low.

Bill checked the progress of his business on a regular basis, comparing the actual results with the budgeted figures. He quickly realised that with the poor sales he was unable to cover his costs. He decided to discuss this with his workforce. They agreed to accept short time working if it meant the survival of the business during the sticky patch, and their jobs would be safe for when business picked up.

George, on the other hand, managed his business in a more haphazard manner. 'We've had bad times before and pulled through,' he would say. He did not realise that as each day went by he was losing more money. The final straw came when the VAT was due at the end of the quarter. He did not have the cash to pay the liability and the bank would not fund him. Eventually his business went bust.

Bill's business survived and his staff are now working full time once again.

SUMMARY

- You must not only *plan* the strategy for your business but you must ensure that you *achieve* the intended goal. This involves checking your progress and taking corrective action when necessary.

- Complete the *actual* columns on your budgeted profit and loss account and your cashflow and compare the results with the projected figures.

- Cashflow problems may not be caused by too few sales or too many costs – they may arise from *timing* problems where customers are taking excessive periods of credit.

- Chase your overdue debtors for payment. If this is done in a reasonable and polite manner then they will respect you for doing so. Indeed, if you do not chase them for payment they will take you for a fool!

- Monitor your gross profit carefully. An error in the pricing of your sales could erode your intended profit margin and mean that there is insufficient contribution from sales to cover overheads.

- Overheads tend to be more stable than trading costs, and therefore easier to forecast. You may only need to verify your overheads three or four times a year to check that they are on target.

- Review your stock levels. Don't carry excessive stock — you will only tie up funds that could be put to a better purpose.

- Use the accounting ratios to monitor the progress of your business. Try to find the **industry standards** for your particular type of business and compare them with your own business.

9
Using Computers to Prepare Budgets & Cashflow Forecasts

Not so very long ago the computer was the exclusive domain of the data processing manager who used the big mainframe computers, but during the 1980s this stranglehold was broken and desktop computers arrived in the shape of the PC (personal computer).

Part of the success of the PC is as a result of **spreadsheet** software that enabled the ordinary person in the street to become a number cruncher. Today spreadsheet software is the second most popular application in personal computing; word processing is first.

By 1990 the spreadsheet market was dominated by a product called **Lotus 1-2-3**. However, since then there has been a huge upsurge in products that run under **Microsoft Windows** and most new computers are now supplied with **Windows 95**. There has also been a move to incorporate spreadsheet programs into suites of software so that data can be easily transferred between integrated database, spreadsheet and word processing applications. An example of this approach is Microsoft Office which includes the program Excel. A further enhancement which is particularly suitable for the Windows environment is the inclusion of sophisticated graphic presentations from the data in the spreadsheets. With these programs you can easily produce pie charts and three dimensional bar graphs. For some years it has been possible to produce elementary graphs from within DOS programs but the modern Windows software allows far greater flexibility.

Today the principal spreadsheet programs running under Windows are **Excel, Quattro Plus** and a **Windows version of Lotus 1-2-3**. DOS-based programs such as the original Lotus 1-2-3 still continue to sell and because their hardware requirements are less they are particularly suitable for older, lower specification PCs.

WHAT IS A SPREADSHEET?

All spreadsheets from the earliest mass program, VisiCalc through to the latest high powered programs are essentially the same. They owe their origins to the accountant's sheet of graph paper pre-printed with rows and columns. In days gone by the budget of even the largest companies would have been prepared by accountants beavering away at those sheets, writing in the figures in pencil and adding up column after column. When the budget didn't work then it was out with the eraser and start again. Today's spreadsheet software still has the same rows and columns but it is now an electronic sheet of paper with the maths calculated in a few microseconds. First of all you plan your spreadsheet; then, when you make a change, all the corresponding figures are automatically adjusted without any hassle.

HOW TO USE A SPREADSHEET

Before you can use the program you must be clear what you wish to achieve. The software is, in itself, no substitute for all the description of budgets and cashflows that has been included earlier in this book: all it does is take the tedious maths from the task and make it easy to adjust as necessary.

Although the keystrokes or mouse movements will vary, the principle behind spreadsheet software is always the same. When you start the program you are confronted with a huge electronic page divided into columns down the page and rows across. Typically there can be up to 256 columns and 8192 rows so you can see it would be a *big* sheet of paper. The computer screen is a 'window' that allows you to look at any small part of the large sheet, and to modify any of the figures and formulas.

Across the top of the worksheet are letters to identify the columns. These are A, B, C... X, Y, Z, AA, AB, AC... AX, AY, AZ etc. Down the side of the sheet are the row numbers. In this way the whole sheet is divided into a maximum of 2,097,152 cells, each of which can be 'addressed' by specifying the column and row number. Thus the 3rd cell down in the 4th column is called D3. This is a little like the game of Battleships & Cruisers that you may have played as a child (see figure 26).

Each cell on the spreadsheet can contain either data (number or text) or a formula. The formula may for example be an instruction to add the numbers from cell D3 to cell C9 and show the answer in

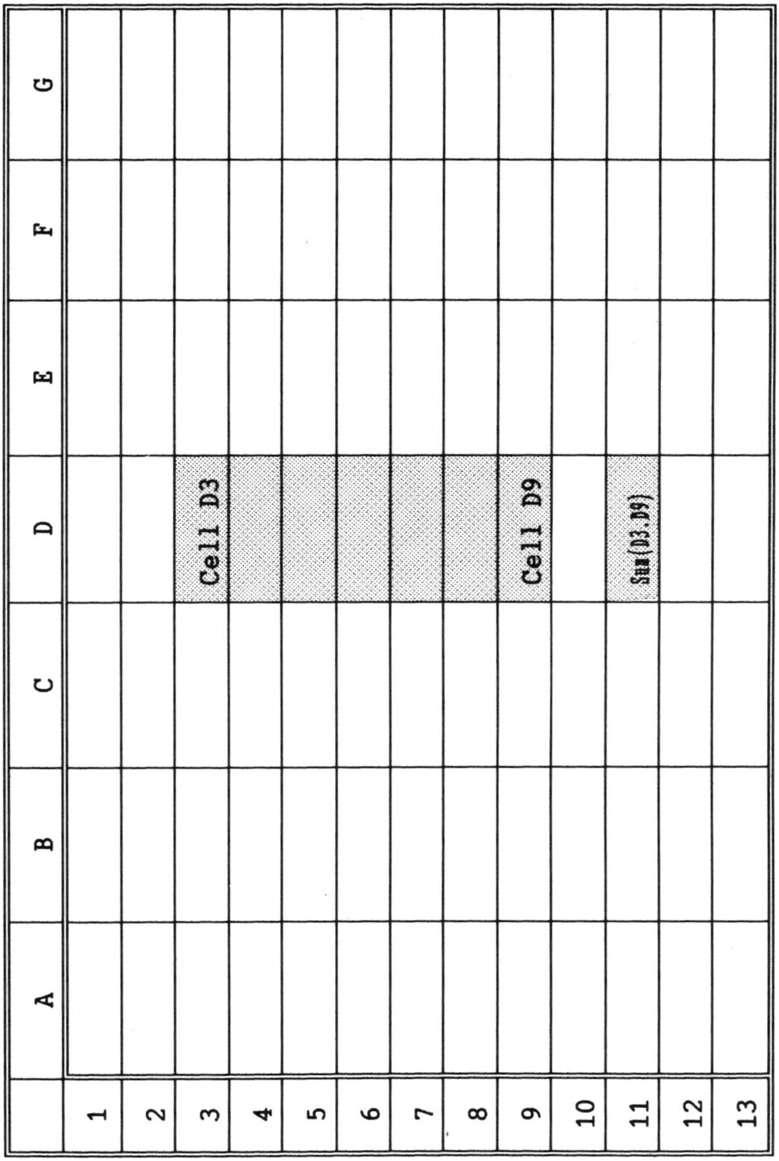

A spreadsheet program

Fig. 26. Illustration to show the cells on the worksheet. Each cell can contain either data (text or numbers) or a formula to tell the worksheet what to do. So for example if cells D3 to D9 contained numbers they would be added together and the total would appear where the formula is entered at D11.

the cell containing the formula (D11). Or it may be just to repeat the value of cell J11 at H9. Many maths functions are supported. In this way you can build up the whole of your budget model and cashflow on the electronic paper.

All the cross references are made electronically on the worksheet, so if the value is altered at one point it is automatically altered throughout the worksheet (without the need for an eraser or Tipp-ex).

When you have finished you can print out the sheet so that is ready to be presented to your bankers. As each program is different it would be impossible in this book to go into all of the ins and outs of spreadsheet programming but the manuals supplied with the software should guide you through this stage.

THE PROS AND CONS OF USING SPREADSHEETS

Advantages
There are many advantages of using such a program. Amongst them are:

- Once you have mastered the skills needed for the program it is quick to use.

- It removes the tedious maths with its inherent possibilities of mistakes through the 'human error'.

- It is easy to modify the budget.

- Because it is so easy to modify the budget it is possible to use 'what if' scenarios and see quickly what the effect of a particular action would be.

- It is possible to introduce 'management by exception' to highlight where things are going wrong.

But you should consider the disadvantages as well.

Disadvantages

- You will not be so deeply involved in the mechanics of preparing the forecasts and so you could make an error without realising. This may be in one of the formulas or could be in the entry of the data.

- You need to acquire a working knowledge of the spreadsheet software so that you can program the model.

Other points on using spreadsheets

One point to make is that when the figures are printed out by the computer they look neat and presentable. Unfortunately this can lull you into a false sense of security — because it looks so good you are given the impression that it must be right, but the old computer maxim 'Rubbish in — rubbish out' still applies and so you must treat the printout with caution until you have fully reviewed it and confirmed that the details are as you would expect.

However, assuming that you have the necessary skills to use the software (and a computer) then the advantages probably outweigh the disadvantages.

When you prepare the budget and cashflow remember to make provision to add the *actual* figures at a later date so that you can monitor the progress of your business.

WHICH SPREADSHEET SOFTWARE SHOULD I USE?

The choice of software will depend, at least in part, on the computer that you have available. If you are already familiar with one spreadsheet program then use that — it will save the learning process necessary to use a new program.

If you are having to purchase a program then give consideration to what you require the program to achieve. Much modern software is full of 'bells and whistles' which you may never use. Software is available for most makes of computer. For the IBM compatible PC, it will depend partly on the specification of the machine: Windows programs typically require at least 4 mb of memory, while 8 mb is recommended for some programs. By contrast, some DOS programs will run with as little as 512 kb of memory.

If you use DOS then a program such as **Lotus 1-2-3 v4** will perhaps meet your needs — it costs around £275. For Windows users you could try one of the following:

- **Excel v5.0** — Microsoft — cost about £225.

- **Quattro Pro v6.0** — Novell — cost about £150.

- **Lotus 1-2-3 for Windows v5.0** — cost about £220.

However, if you consider that your use of the program may be limited then do not rule out Shareware programs such as **As-Easy-As v7.0**, a Lotus 1-2-3 clone. This will cost about £60 and although much cheaper than its rivals and without some of the features, it is first class software and well worth looking at.

CONCLUSION

The use of computers in preparing budgets and cashflows is to be recommended provided that they are used with a degree of caution. Remember, unless you know what you are trying to accomplish, and know how to achieve the task manually, then you will not be able to arrive at the right result using a computer. If you do know what you are doing then the use of a spreadsheet program for this type of task can save a lot of time and allow you to try out 'what if' scenarios.

10
Budgeting for All

So far we have considered the role of budgets and cashflows in relation to businesses but the same techniques can be equally applied to other types of organisation. In an increasingly complex world it is becoming even more important that the administrators of public service organisations appreciate the benefits and pitfalls of budgets and cashflows in relation to them. Budgets can of course be prepared for clubs and societies, charities, local councils or national organisations. Each type of entity presents its own problems but by way of example we will consider schools and hospitals.

MANAGING SCHOOL BUDGETS

Schools in the public sector present a special case in that the vast majority of their income is fixed by an outside organisation — usually the Local Education Authority (LEA). It is then for the school to juggle with the way in which it spends the money in order to achieve the educational aims.

Under the recent Education Acts the way in which each school spends its allocation of funds is now the responsibility of the governors. This is known as **Local Management of Schools** (LMS). In theory the governors are free to decide how the money is spent but in practice, with the social and community pressures imposed upon the school, there is relatively little room for manoeuvre. Arrangements will vary slightly from one LEA to another but in general they will broadly follow the outline set out below.

A few schools have a cheque book and can make their own payments. But most schools will make the decision as to what is purchased and what staff are employed, while the funds are held centrally by the LEA and it is the LEA which makes the actual payment. The schools merely receive the invoice for the goods and after approving it pass the document to the LEA to be paid.

125

Schools are usually notified of their income allocation in early spring for the financial year starting 1st April. They are then obliged to prepare a budget showing how they propose to use the money, have the budget approved by the governors and then submit a copy to the LEA. During the year the LEA monitors what is happening. Regular reports are produced to show how the school is actually spending its money in comparison with the budget.

Apart from the income from the LEA — which in turn comes from a combination of central government grants and local council tax — the school is free to raise extra funds through voluntary contributions and from the renting out of the school premises. In practice these extra funds only account for a very small proportion of the total income.

Main headings of a school budget

The budget will be prepared under the following headings:

Employee Costs	88.6%
Capitation (Books & Materials)	2.8%
Premises Related Costs	3.7%
Transport Related Costs	0.1%
Supplies & Services (Insurance,	
Telephone & Exam Fees etc)	3.8%
	99.0%
Less Income from Lettings	(0.9%)
	98.1%
Fund Reserves – brought forward	
from earlier year	1.9%
TOTAL FUNDS AVAILABLE	100.0%

The percentages show the typical amount of each class of expenditure compared with the total funds available. As you will see the vast majority of the budget goes on staffing costs.

Normally capital expenditure on school buildings is not delegated to the school, but remains under the direct control of the LEA. The LEA as landlord also keeps responsibility for the *major* structural building related costs.

How a school budget is prepared

The financial year for schools runs from 1st April to the following

31st March. This does not coincide with the academic year, which runs from 1st September to the following 31st August. The income allocation for each school is calculated by a formula which takes account of the number of pupils, their age, and also the structure of the school buildings. For example a greater allowance is made for year 12 and 13 students than for pupils in year 9. The formula also recognises that larger school premises cost more to heat and repair than smaller ones.

When looking at pupil numbers the income allocation is initially based upon the numbers in the school at September before the start of the financial year (see figure 27). If student numbers are rising, and the extra pupils join the school in September, it is not until the following April that the school receives any additional funding (although exceptions are made if there is an extraordinarily high increase in numbers). On the other hand if numbers are declining then the school receives an excessive allocation!

During the Autumn term the school gathers information about the likely number of pupils that will be joining the school the following September. Each school has a **standard number**, the maximum number of new pupils it can be asked to accommodate in any year. This at least sets an upper limit on the number of pupils in the school. The next step is to build up the **needs budget**. From the forecast number of pupils it is possible to calculate the number of teachers that will be needed and in turn from this the amount of teaching salaries. Forecasts are also prepared for the other categories of expense to arrive at the total funds that the school considers that it needs.

Then the *actual* income allocation is notified to the school which may throw the needs budget into chaos! There may be some scope for minor savings in other areas, but the dominance of salary costs means this must be the main category for cost saving. Often this can only be achieved by reducing the number or hours of teaching staff and making larger classes. Careful review of the timetable may also produce some additional teaching hours to lessen the effect on the students.

One other idea which has been put forward in some schools is to replace senior staff with teachers new from teacher training college. I will leave you to judge the merits of this, but from a financial viewpoint the benefits are obvious. A teacher who has been in the profession for many years will be on a higher salary than one who is only just embarking on their career.

Once the budget plan has been drawn up it is passed to the

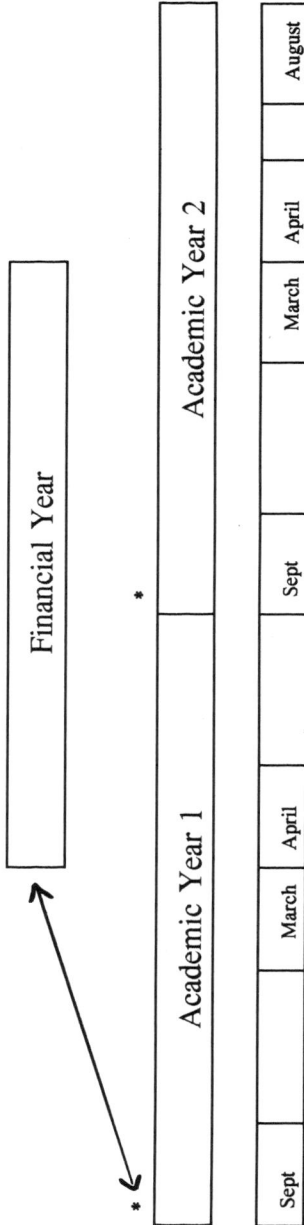

Fig. 27. The school budgeting periods.

governors for their approval. When they have given their OK a copy is passed to the LEA as the financial plan for the school for the ensuing year. During the year reports will be prepared (see figure 28) so that the actual progress can be monitored. If savings have been made and the expenditure in one area appears to be running below budget then, with the governors' approval, it is possible to 'vire' (transfer) the surplus to another area where expenditure is behaving less kindly.

In this way the budget is modified throughout the year in the light of the actual expenditure taking place. Under the LMS the LEA's role has been reduced to a 'watching brief' to ensure that the schools do not get into trouble but the day to day decision making has been passed to the schools. One final point to make is that, unless the school is maintaining its own bank account, there will normally be no need for the school to bother about cashflow. Provided that the school does not exceed its total expenditure target for the year there is normally no restriction as to *when* the money is spent. However since most is spent on teachers' salaries, this has the effect of spreading the expenditure fairly evenly over the period.

One of the difficulties in preparing the budget for a school is to strike the right balance between financial constraints and the social consequences arising from the decisions made. Unlike a business which is run to make a profit, the primary objective of a school is to educate the pupils and this must never be overlooked. After all a school with no pupils would not require teachers and with that expense saved it would almost certainly run with a large budget surplus — but it would not be serving the needs of the community or achieving its social aims.

MANAGING HOSPITAL BUDGETS

A private hospital presents its own set of problems to the producer of a budget. With hospitals it is the number of patients and the procedures that they require which determines hospital revenue. A hospital administrator once said, 'the ideal patient is one who comes on 1st January, stays for a year, and goes to theatre for an operation every day. Those are the most profitable for us but we don't get many of those!'

Most patients at a private hospital are members of one of the medical benefit schemes such as BUPA or PPP. There are normally two aspects to their treatment; the procedure carried out by the consultant, and the provision of the hospital accommodation with

----

Fund: LEA General Fund   Allocation   Expenditure Variance

Heading: Employees	Allocation	Expenditure	Variance
Bud/Acc: Teaching Staff	1648240.00	831926.68	-816313.32
Bud/Acc: Non Teaching Staff	99530.00	48617.80	-50912.20
Bud/Acc: Supply/Additional Hours	5000.00	765.42	-4234.58
Bud/Acc: Hourly Paid Staff	7500.00	3371.84	-4128.16
Bud/Acc: Other Employee Expenses	2000.00	125.87	-1874.13
Bud/Acc: Caretaking	36168.00	17897.37	-18270.63
Sub total	1798438.00	902704.98	-895733.02

Heading: Capitation	Allocation	Expenditure	Variance
Bud/Acc: Capitation	56866.00	36976.19	-19889.81
Sub total	56866.00	36976.19	-19889.81

Heading: Premises Related Costs	Allocation	Expenditure	Variance
Bud/Acc: Repairs & Maintenance	13250.00	7134.98	-6115.02
Bud/Acc: Heating & Lighting	48000.00	16880.33	-31119.67
Bud/Acc: Cleaning Materials	1000.00	439.54	-560.46
Bud/Acc: Water Services	11750.00	2427.14	-9322.86
Sub total	74000.00	26881.99	-47118.01

Heading: Transport Related Costs	Allocation	Expenditure	Variance
Bud/Acc: Vehicle Expenses	220.00	0.00	-220.00
Bud/Acc: Car Allowances	400.00	152.35	-247.65
Sub total	620.00	152.35	-467.65

Heading: Supplies and Services	Allocation	Expenditure	Variance
Bud/Acc: Educational Equipment	9000.00	6084.38	-2915.62
Bud/Acc: Non Educ. Equip./Services	11750.00	5593.45	-6156.55
Bud/Acc: Communications	6000.00	3150.41	-2849.59
Bud/Acc: Examination Fees	47000.00	46404.50	-595.50
Bud/Acc: Insurance - All Risks	2950.00	2950.75	0.75
Bud/Acc: Educ. Visits	4000.00	3027.39	-972.61
Sub total	80700.00	67210.88	-13489.12

Heading: Income	Allocation	Expenditure	Variance
Bud/Acc: Income	-18904.00	-5870.55	13033.45
Sub total	-18904.00	-5870.55	13033.45

Fund Reserves (unallocated)	39100.78		-39100.78
FUND TOTALS	2030820.78	-1028055.84	-1002764.94

Fig. 28. The school budget report.

130

its supporting services. In 95% of cases the consultant is paid directly by the patient or his medical scheme: the consultant is not paid by the hospital. The hospital charges the patient for general nursing care, use of facilities such as operating theatres, pathology departments etc and consumables such as drugs and dressings.

In practice the hospital will forecast patient activity, splitting the patients between day patients and in-patients. This will be done from local historical data if available. If it is a new hospital then the forecast will be as a result of market research having considered the availability of consultants, waiting lists in the public sector, and so on. Local data has to be used in all the estimates because the types of activity will vary from hospital to hospital. This is because different National Health hospitals have different specialities. The consultants who work within the National Health Service are often the same consultants who provide the service to the private hospitals. Thus a private hospital in Leicester will probably be able to provide a cardiac service because the National Health hospitals in that area employ a considerable number of heart specialists who are therefore also available to the private sector.

The different types of patient make different demands on the hospital facilities. Day patients use a lot of the hospital services, but do not require room occupancy, whereas in-patients require both.

The next step is to forecast the types of procedure to be undertaken. This is most important. For example procedures may be orthopaedic, ENT or gynaecological. The type of procedure being undertaken will affect the expected length of stay, and so this is also taken into account when calculating the number of **patient days** for accommodation purposes. The actual facilities at the hospital will rarely be a limiting factor in the amount of patients. Normally there will be a substantial over capacity in this area because on the room occupancy the hospital will still be able to run at a profit with less than 50% usage. Planned use of operating theatres etc will normally be during the day but there is nothing to stop them being used until, say, 3.00 in the morning if the demand is there. The limiting factor is usually the availability of consultants. If more consultants move into an area then the forecast would be adjusted upwards to recognise this fact.

Returning to the types of procedure, the **case mix** will determine the demands made upon the ancillary services of the hospital. Therefore once the expected case mix is established the usage of the departments can be forecast. These departments will include:

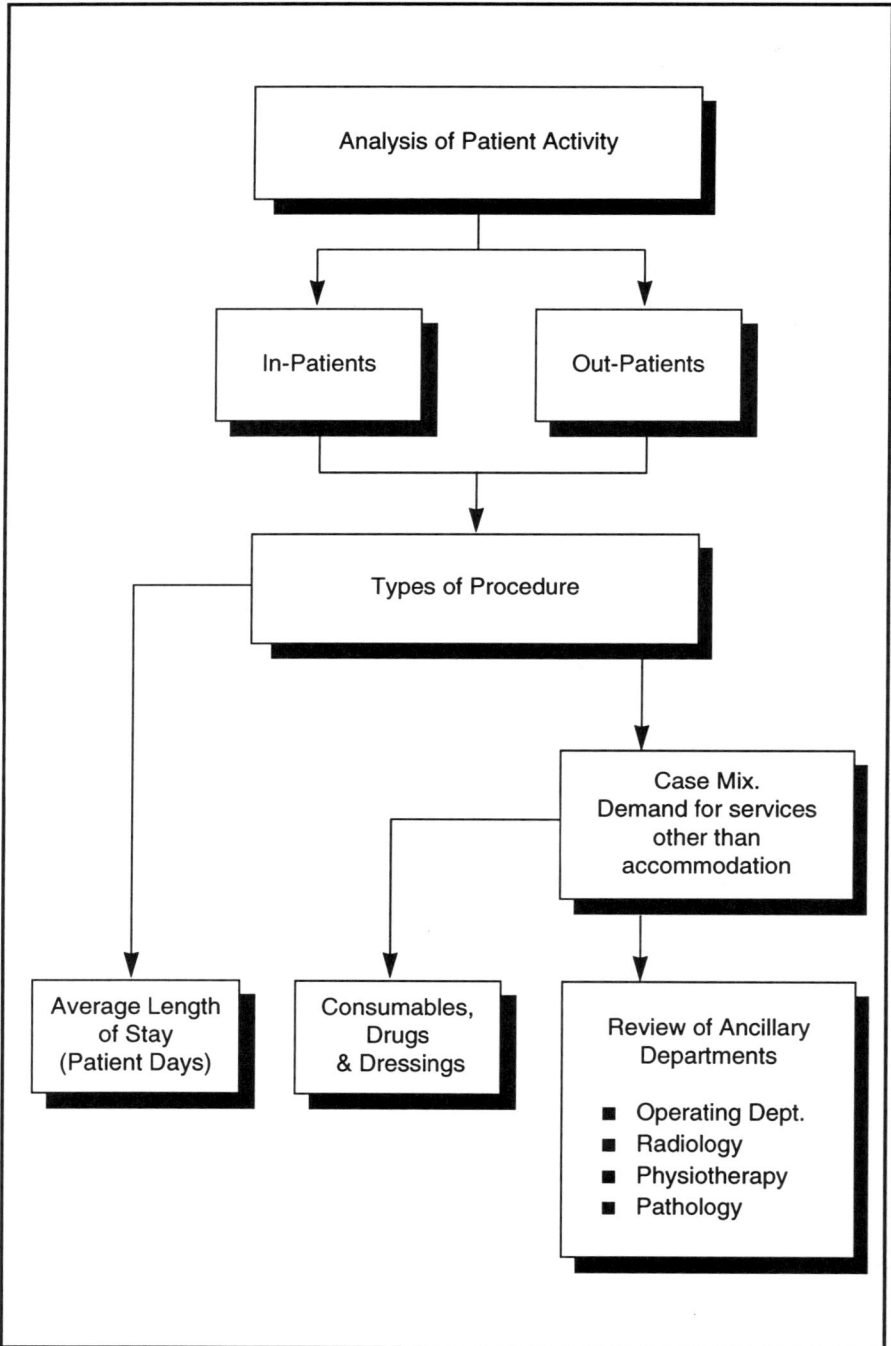

Fig. 29. The budget process for a private hospital.

Operating departments
Radiology
Physiotherapy
Pathology

The demand for drugs and dressings etc can also be calculated. Once the demand for each service has been established then the financial budget can be started. Income and costs from each activity should be calculated to establish their contribution towards the overall revenue of the hospital. Even this is not quite straightforward, because for example different medical schemes pay different rates for accommodation for the same room. The hospital needs to forecast the number of patients from each medical scheme as well as the overall number of patients.

The room rates etc will be negotiated each year with the various medical insurers. Items such as drugs will have a mark-up applied, which (depending upon the nature of the item) may be from 15% to 200%.

Having calculated the contributions from each activity, general overheads applying to the hospital as a whole will be deducted. These will include administration salaries, repairs to the structure of the building, and heating and power. If the hospital is part of a group then there will also be a deduction for the group head office costs before arriving at the forecast surplus for the year.

In some respects the hospital is like any other business. Income is forecast from the various different sources and the expenditure for each cost centre is calculated to establish the contribution towards the overall surplus or profit. Unlike schools the cashflow is most important to monitor as well as the budget.

HOUSEHOLD BUDGETS

Finally, these same techniques can also be applied to your personal household budget. You can forecast your income from your salary and other sources, and your household expenditure, and work out whether you really can afford that extra holiday that you have promised yourself. Just like the business, cashflow is important — your bank manager will consider it vital even if you don't!

Obviously the headings that you will use will be different and it is often difficult to decide what headings you will need. By way of suggestion consider:

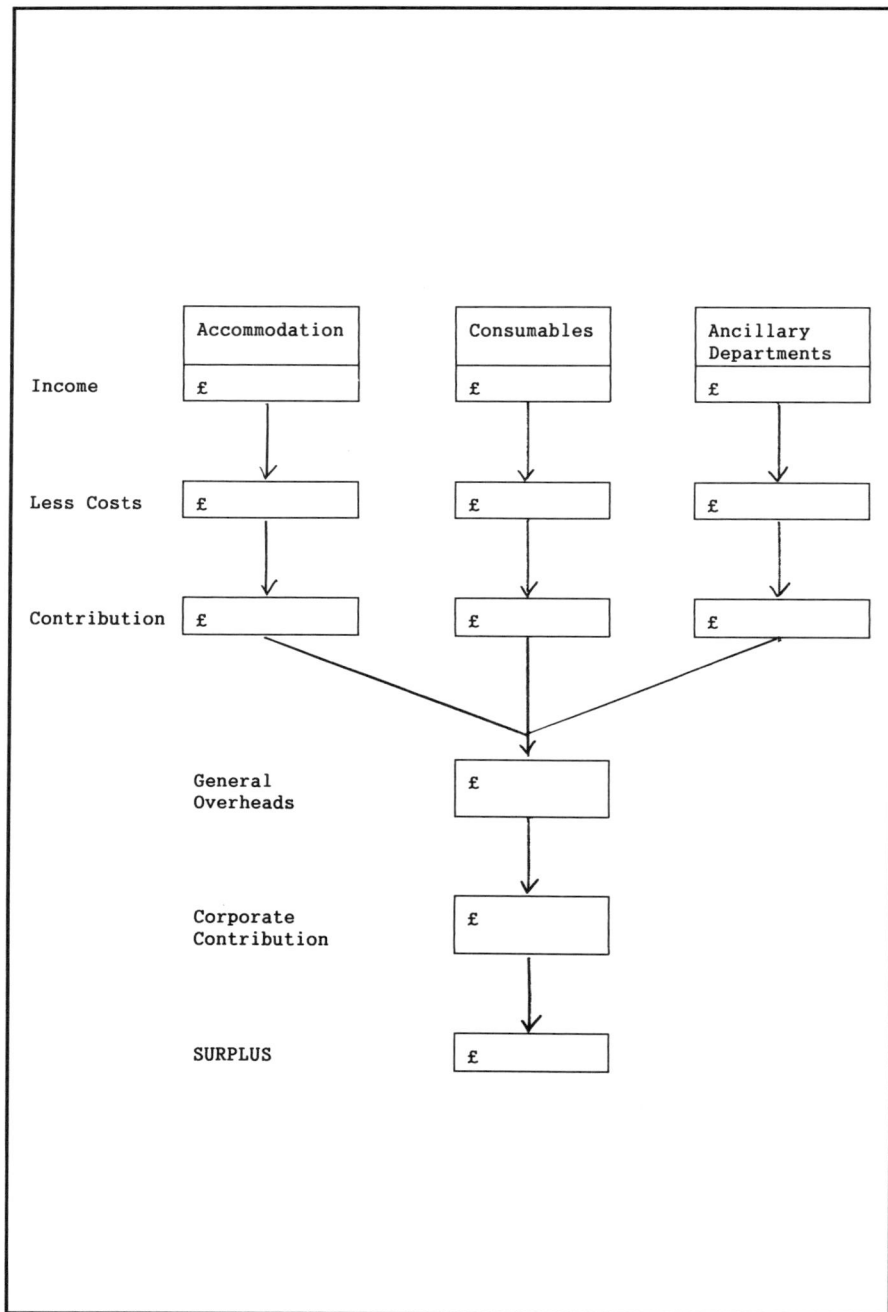

Fig. 30. Building up the figures for a private hospital budget.

Income
Salary or pension
Bank and/or building society interest
Other income

Expenditure
Food
Clothing
Mortgage repayments or rent
Council tax and water
Fuel – electricity, gas, coal etc
Household insurance
Car expenses
Life insurance
Holidays
Other expenses

This will give you a starting point but you will soon think of some extra useful headings. The techniques for preparing the budget and the cashflow are essentially the same as those we have already discussed in relation to businesses.

One point to mention concerning household accounts is that those of you who have a personal computer may find a program such as 'Page Cheque Book' (from Shareware — see appendix 4) useful in keeping track of your bank account. This will not actually assist you to forecast your total expenditure for the year ahead but it will help you to record where the money has gone. It will also assist you in checking your bank statement. Using the 'look forward' facility you can make sure that you have enough money in the account to meet your standing order payments later in the month.

CASE STUDY

John had been a teacher for many years but he had been taken ill and advised by his doctor not to return to teaching. Although the school had continued to pay his salary at the full rate for six months this was now to be cut to half rate and it would stop altogether after he had been ill for a year. At this stage it might be possible for him to obtain early retirement on ill health grounds, and if so he would then receive a reduced pension.

In addition to his teaching, John had run a part time business making pottery and his wife Diana also had a small part time job.

John decided to discuss his finances with a friend and between them they drew up the family budget as follows:

The Brocklehurst Family Budget

Income	*Monthly*
John – salary	1180
Diana – salary	220
Child benefit	110
Business profits (pottery) - £1800 pa	150
	1660

Expenditure

Mortgage	765
Property insurance	21
Property repairs	20
Life insurance	50
Council tax	46
Electricity	30
Telephone	28
Heating (coal & logs)	30
Water	8
Motor expenses – repairs, road tax & insurance	70
fuel – £25 pw	108
Food – £60pw	260
Cash expenses – £35 pw	152
Clothing	40
Bank charges	10
TV licence	7
	1645

Surplus	15

Note: Expenses have been averaged over 12 months — some months may have heavy expenditure whilst others are light.

It was clear that the budget only just balanced when John was on his full salary. What could be done?

It turned out that the mortgage incorporated a **protection scheme** which would pay £220 per month towards the mortgage. In addition a halving of the gross salary would not mean a halving of the spendable amount. Because of tax and national insurance it would only reduce to about two thirds of the full salary.

These, together with other such matters, would mean that the family could scrape by. They also prepared an Action Plan which included amongst other things:

- establishing the rights to invalidity pension

- building up the pottery business

- reorganising the banking arrangements to save interest and charges.

SUMMARY

- Budgets can be prepared for many different types of organisation — not just businesses but schools, hospitals, and domestic households.

- Schools budgets are dominated by teachers' salaries.

- Just like a business (which in essence is what it is) a hospital needs to split its income into the different procedures (products) that it can offer and assess the income from each.

- Household budgets and cashflows can be prepared along the same lines — they just need different titles for the categories of income and expenditure.

Appendix 1
Loan Repayment Table
Interest & Capital

MONTHLY GROSS REPAYMENT (£) PER £1000.00 BORROWED (QUARTERLY INTEREST)

NOMINAL INTEREST RATE %	TERM IN YEARS												
	1	2	3	4	5	6	7	8	9	10	15	20	25
7.0	86.50	44.75	30.85	23.92	19.78	17.02	15.07	13.61	12.48	11.59	8.96	7.72	7.04
7.5	86.73	44.97	31.08	24.15	20.01	17.26	15.31	13.86	12.73	11.84	9.24	8.02	7.35
8.0	86.96	45.20	31.31	24.38	20.25	17.50	15.55	14.10	12.99	12.10	9.52	8.33	7.68
8.5	87.19	45.42	31.53	24.62	20.48	17.74	15.80	14.36	13.24	12.36	9.81	8.64	8.01
9.0	87.42	45.65	31.76	24.85	20.72	17.99	16.05	14.61	13.50	12.63	10.10	8.95	8.34
9.5	87.64	45.88	31.99	25.08	20.96	18.23	16.30	14.87	13.76	12.89	10.39	9.27	8.68
10.0	87.87	46.10	32.22	25.32	21.20	18.48	16.55	15.13	14.03	13.16	10.69	9.59	9.02
10.5	88.10	46.33	32.45	25.55	21.44	18.73	16.81	15.39	14.30	13.44	10.99	9.92	9.37
11.0	88.33	46.56	32.69	25.79	21.69	18.98	17.07	15.65	14.57	13.71	11.30	10.25	9.72
11.5	88.56	46.78	32.92	26.03	21.93	19.23	17.32	15.92	14.84	13.99	11.61	10.58	10.08
12.0	88.79	47.01	33.15	26.27	22.18	19.48	17.58	16.18	15.11	14.27	11.92	10.92	10.44
12.5	89.02	47.24	33.39	26.51	22.43	19.74	17.85	16.45	15.39	14.56	12.24	11.27	10.80
13.0	89.25	47.47	33.62	26.75	22.68	20.00	18.11	16.72	15.67	14.84	12.56	11.61	11.17
13.5	89.48	47.70	33.86	27.00	22.93	20.25	18.38	17.00	15.95	15.13	12.88	11.96	11.54
14.0	89.71	47.93	34.09	27.24	23.18	20.52	18.65	17.28	16.24	15.43	13.20	12.31	11.91
14.5	89.94	48.16	34.33	27.49	23.43	20.78	18.92	17.55	16.52	15.72	13.53	12.67	12.28
15.0	90.17	48.39	34.57	27.73	23.69	21.04	19.19	17.83	16.81	16.02	13.87	13.03	12.66
15.5	90.40	48.63	34.81	27.98	23.94	21.31	19.46	18.12	17.10	16.32	14.20	13.39	13.04
16.0	90.63	48.86	35.05	28.23	24.20	21.57	19.74	18.40	17.39	16.62	14.54	13.75	13.42
16.5	90.86	49.09	35.29	28.48	24.46	21.84	20.02	18.69	17.69	16.92	14.88	14.12	13.80
17.0	91.09	49.32	35.53	28.73	24.72	22.11	20.30	18.98	17.99	17.23	15.22	14.48	14.19
17.5	91.32	49.56	35.77	28.98	24.98	22.38	20.58	19.27	18.29	17.53	15.56	14.85	14.57
18.0	91.55	49.79	36.02	29.23	25.25	22.65	20.86	19.56	18.59	17.84	15.91	15.23	14.96
19.0	92.02	50.27	36.51	29.75	25.78	23.21	21.43	20.15	19.20	18.48	16.61	15.98	15.74
20.0	92.48	50.74	37.00	30.26	26.31	23.76	22.01	20.75	19.82	19.11	17.32	16.73	16.52

Appendix 2
Loan Repayment Table
Interest Only

INTEREST ONLY LOANS
QUARTERLY INTEREST REPAYMENTS (£) PER £1000.00 BORROWED

Nominal Interest Rate (%)	Quarterly Interest Repayment (£)	Nominal Interest Rate (%)	Quarterly Interest Repayment (£)	Nominal Interest Rate (%)	Quarterly Interest Repayment (£)
7.0	17.50	11.5	28.75	16.0	40.00
7.5	18.75	12.0	30.00	16.5	41.25
8.0	20.00	12.5	31.25	17.0	42.50
8.5	21.25	13.0	32.50	17.5	43.75
9.0	22.50	13.5	33.75	18.0	45.00
9.5	23.75	14.0	35.00	18.5	46.25
10.0	25.00	14.5	36.25	19.0	47.50
10.5	26.25	15.0	37.50	19.5	48.75
11.0	27.50	15.5	38.75	20.0	50.00

% Price Change	Existing Gross Profit %									
	5	10	15	20	25	30	35	40	45	50
15	-75	-60	-50	-43	-38	-33	-30	-27	-25	-23
12.5	-71	-56	-45	-38	-33	-29	-26	-24	-22	-20
10	-67	-50	-40	-33	-29	-25	-22	-20	-18	-17
7.5	-60	-43	-33	-27	-23	-20	-18	-16	-14	-13
5	-50	-33	-25	-20	-17	-14	-13	-11	-10	-9
4	-44	-29	-21	-17	-14	-12	-10	-9	-8	-7
3	-38	-23	-17	-13	-11	-9	-8	-7	-6	-6
2	-29	-17	-12	-9	-7	-6	-5	-5	-4	-4
1	-17	-9	-6	-5	-4	-3	-3	-2	-2	-2
0	0	0	0	0	0	0	0	0	0	0
-1	25	11	7	5	4	3	3	3	2	2
-2	67	25	15	11	9	7	6	5	5	4
-3	150	43	25	18	14	11	9	8	7	6
-4	400	67	36	25	19	15	13	11	10	9
-5	0	100	50	33	25	20	17	14	13	11
-7.5	0	300	100	60	43	33	27	23	20	18
-10	0	0	200	100	67	50	40	33	29	25
-12.5	0	0	500	167	100	71	56	45	38	33
-15	0	0	0	300	150	100	75	60	50	43

The table shows the increase or reduction in sales volume that is needed to maintain the same level of profits following a change in the price charged. For example if the existing rate of profit is 20% and there is a 7.5% reduction in selling price you will need to increase the sales volume by 60% to maintain the same margin.

Appendix 4
Sources of Computer Software

The software mentioned in Chapter 9 can be obtained from most computer stores or by mail order. Look for the adverts in magazines such as *Personal Computer World*. If you need to contact the suppliers of the programs their telephone numbers are as follows;

Microsoft   (01734) 270000

Novell   (01344) 724000

Lotus   (01784) 455445

If you are new to computing, you may need help in deciding which program will best serve your needs. In this case a trip to your local specialist computer store is probably the best course of action. They should be able to describe the various features of each program and it is likely that you will be able to see the software running and get some *hands on* experience before you commit yourself to the purchase. Stores such as **PC World** and **Escom** have nationwide chains of outlets, each with a wide selection of computer hardware and software. To find the nearest store contact PC World on (0990) 464464 or Escom on (0990) 555888.

SHAREWARE

An alternative source of software is shareware. Shareware is copyrighted and patented software that is marketed on a 'try before you buy' basis. You can get a copy of the program for a nominal fee of around £3.00 per disk and try the software for a trial period, generally 30 days, without obligation. At this stage you are not provided with manuals but generally you can print yourself a provisional manual from information on the disks. You must pay the full price for the software only if you continue to use it after the end of the trial period. If it doesn't meet your needs, you discard it and try something else. That is not to say that all Shareware is of the same quality — some is rubbish — but it has not cost a fortune to try it.

A shareware program that may be of interest for those starting to prepare budgets and cash flows is the spreadsheet program **As-Easy-As**. To find out more about shareware contact Atlantic Coast PLC on (01297) 552222.

Glossary

Accounting concepts

A set of rules governing the preparation of accounts. The four accounting concepts are:

- The Going Concern Concept
- The Accruals Concept
- The Consistency Concept
- The Prudence Concept

For more details see page 31.

Accounting ratios

A set of ratios to help unravel the true meaning of the figures disclosed in the accounts. Instead of looking at the figures themselves it is often useful to express the ratio or percentage of one figure compared with another and by doing so it is easier to make inter-business comparisons. See page 110 for more details.

Aged debtors list

A summary of the debtor balances (amounts owed to the business by customers) analysed to reveal the age of the debts. It is normal to age debts into current month, 30 to 60 days, 60 to 90 days, and over 90 days. This shows clearly which debts are becoming a problem because of non-payment and therefore which need chasing.

Analytical review

A critical review of the progress of the business comparing the results for the current accounting period against the results of earlier accounting periods, or the results of other similar businesses, and the calculation of accounting ratios to reveal the strengths and weaknesses of the business.

Balance sheet

A statement of the worth of the business at the accounting date expressed in terms of historical cost.

Break-even point

The costs of a business are made up of two elements; fixed costs, mainly overheads and variable costs, chiefly related to the level of productive activity. As each unit of the product is produced and sold the difference between the selling price and the variable cost of production is the contribution towards the fixed costs. As activity increases this contribution reaches a point where it exactly equals the fixed costs — the **break-even point**. Beyond this activity level the business will run in profit: below that point it will incur losses.

Budget

A financial and/or quantitative statement, prepared prior to the accounting period, setting the policy to be pursued to achieve the desired goal and against which the progress during the accounting period can be measured so that necessary correcting action can be taken if the actual results are not achieving the stated aims.

Capital expenditure

Expenditure on acquiring fixed assets which will have a lasting benefit to the business. (Contrast revenue expenditure.)

Cash accounting system (for VAT)

A method of accounting for VAT at the time that the monetary transaction for payment of the goods or services takes place. The system is available to traders whose annual turnover is less than £350,000. (Contrast tax point system.)

Cash budget

The forecasting of the movement of cash within the business to ensure that there is adequate finance available. This will involve the preparation of a cashflow forecast (see below).

Cashflow forecast

A schedule showing the budgeted receipts and payments for the forthcoming year (or period). Often there is provision to include the actual amounts received and paid alongside the budgeted figures which aids the monitoring of the results.

Cashflow statement

Another name for the cashflow forecast.

Credit period

The period between the supply and invoicing of goods or services, and the payment of the invoice. If you allow your customers to take credit then you must monitor the credit period (through the use of aged debtors lists) because your business is having to finance those debtors. If the credit period is excessive then your business may run short of cash causing you embarrassment and your bank interest charges may also be exorbitant.

Creditors

The suppliers to the business to whom money is owed and the amount owed by the business to them (contrast debtors).

Current assets

These are assets which are either cash or can be turned into cash quite quickly. They include cash, bank balances (not overdrafts), debtors, stock and work in progress. (Contrast current liabilities and fixed assets.)

Current liabilities

These are amounts owed to suppliers (creditors) together with short term loans such as bank overdrafts. Short term loans are those less than one year and so part of hire purchase liabilities may also be included under this heading where they are repayable within the next twelve months. (Contrast current assets.)

Debtors

The customers of the business who owe money to the business and the amount owed. (Contrast creditors.)

Debtors matrix

Another name for the aged debtors list.

Depreciation

An allowance made (charged as an expense in the profit and loss account) for the reduction in value of fixed assets (particularly machinery, furnishings and motor vehicles) during each accounting period. See page 29 for more details.

Direct costs

Direct costs are those costs directly related to the production of the product. If you are running a clothing factory then the cost of the cloth which is made into garments and the wages of the workers cutting the cloth and sewing the garments would be direct costs. (Contrast indirect costs and overheads.)

Fixed assets

Property and equipment owned by a business which will have a long lasting benefit to the business. Examples would be buildings, plant and machinery, office furnishings and equipment, and motor vehicles. (Contrast current assets.)

Fixed costs

A fixed cost is one which tends to be unaffected by variations in the volume of output. Fixed costs arise mainly with the passing of time and often relate to overheads.

Gross profit

The profit earned by a business from trading, prior to the deduction of overhead expenses. That is to say that sales income less direct costs on those sales equals gross profit (see also net profit).

Indirect costs

Indirect costs are those costs which do not relate directly to the production of the product but which are necessary to provide the setting in which the business is run and to provide the appropriate services for the business. Rent, insurance, salaries of office staff, and bank charges are all examples of indirect costs. These are also referred to as overheads.

Key ratios

It is often difficult to look at the profit and loss account or the balance sheet of a business and get a true picture of what is happening. This is where ratios come in because it is often easier to make more sense of the relationship between two numbers than it is to look at the numbers themselves. Liquidity ratios, profit ratios and efficiency ratios are examples of the key ratios used to review a business. See chapter 8 for more details.

Long term liabilities

Amounts owed by a business which are not due for payment within one year. Liabilities of this nature will tend to be owed to banks on loans or amounts due under hire purchase agreements.

Net assets

Net assets are the total assets of the business minus its liabilities (excluding the proprietor's investment).

Net profit

The profit of a business after taking account of all expenses.

Overheads

Money spent regularly to keep the business running. Overheads include such charges as rent, heat and light, bank interest on overdrafts and other expenses which are not directly related to the purchase of goods or services being sold by the business.

PAYE

(Pay As You Earn) A system for collecting income tax and national insurance contributions by deductions from employees' wages.

Profit and loss account

An account summarising the income and expenditure of a business for a given period and showing the surplus income (profit) or deficit (loss).

Quick assets

This is a subdivision of current assets. Although stocks and work in progress are constantly being realised and converted into cash and are therefore included within current assets, if it came to 'the crunch' these may be hard to sell very quickly. These types of asset are therefore excluded from the definition of 'quick assets' which includes the other current assets such as cash, bank balances and debtors.

Revenue expenditure

The benefit of revenue expenditure is wholly used up within the accounting period in which the expenditure is incurred. Thus the purchase of raw materials, the payment of rent and expenditure on salaries and wages are all examples of revenue expenditure. (Contrast capital expenditure.)

Spreadsheet software

A spreadsheet is an 'electronic piece of paper' divided into rows and columns. By entering formulas into the spreadsheet it is possible for the program to carry out mathematical functions such as 'add up a column and put the total here' in a matter of microseconds. If any changes are made to the figures on the spreadsheet it is automatically recalculated to show the new answer. (See chapter 9 for more detail.)

Standard rate (of VAT)

The rate at which VAT is charged on most transactions — currently 17.5%.

Tax point system (for VAT)

The tax point system of accounting for VAT is to record the transaction for VAT purposes at the time that the goods or services are invoiced regardless as to whether they have or have not been paid for. If your annual turnover is in excess of £350,000 you must adopt this basis: if less you can use cash accounting if you wish.

Variable costs

Variable costs are those costs which vary in amount along with the level of activity of the business. They will include the direct production costs but will exclude overhead costs such as rent etc.

VAT (Value Added Tax)

A tax on consumer spending. The tax (currently at 17.5%) is levied on the sales/supplies made by registered traders. Because of the set-off of tax charged to the trader on his purchases the effect is that each trader accounts for the tax on the value added by him — see chapter 3 for more detail.

Further Reading

The Barclays Guide to Financial Management for the Small Business, Peter Wilson (Blackwell Publishers, 1990).

Bigg's Cost Accounts, 11th edition, J Wald (Pitman, 1984).

The Business Plan Workbook, Colin and Paul Barrow (Kogan Page Ltd, 1988).

Business Planning & Development, a Practical Guide, Bill Elsom (First Class Publishing, Doncaster).

Cashflow & How To Improve It, Leon Hopkins (Kogan Page Publishers, 1993).

Financial Handbook for Sales & Marketing Managers, Anthony Taylor and Keith Steward (Cassell Educational Ltd, 1990).

First Course in Cost & Management Accounting, T Lucey (D P Publicatons, 1990).

How to Keep Business Accounts, Peter Taylor (How To Books Ltd, 3rd edition 1994).

How to Master Book-Keeping, Peter Marshall (How To Books, 2nd edition 1995).

How to Prepare a Business Plan, Matthew Record (How To Books, 1995).

How to Start Your Own Business, Jim Green (How To Books, 1995).

How to Understand Finance at Work, Peter Marshall (How To Books, 1994).

Lloyds Bank Small Business Guide, 1994 edition, Sara Williams (Penguin Books, 1993).

The Perfect Business Plan, Ron Johnson (Century Business, 1993).

Perfect Financial Ratios, Terry Gasking (Century Business, 1993).

Small Business Finance — A simple approach (NatWest Business Handbook) John Lambden & David Targett (Pitman Publishing, 1993).

Useful Addresses

Association of British Chambers of Commerce
Sovereign House
212 Shaftesbury Avenue
London WC2H 8EW

Tel: (0171) 240 5831

Association of Independent Business
Ilford House
133-135 Oxford Street
London W1R 1TD

Tel: (0171) 287 6115

British Technology Group
101 Newington Causeway
London SE1 6BU

Tel: (0171) 403 6666

Business in the Community
227a City Road
London EC1V 1LX

Tel: (0171) 253 3716

Chartered Association of Certified Accountants
29 Lincoln's Inn Fields
London WC2A 3EE

Tel: (0171) 242 6855

Companies Registration Office
Companies House
Crown Way, Maindy
Cardiff CF4 3UZ

Tel: (01222) 388588

Confederation of British Industry
Centrepoint
103 New Oxford Street
London WC1A 1DU

Tel: (0171) 379 7400

Department of Trade and Industry (DTI)
1-19 Victoria Street
London SW1H 0ET

Tel: (0171) 215 7877

Federation of Crafts and Commerce
Federation House
Rodney Road
Southsea
Hants PO4 8SY

Tel: (01705) 817224

Health & Safety Executive
Baynards House
1 Chepstow Place
Westbourne Grove
London W2 4TF

Tel: (0171) 221 0870

Institute of Chartered Accountants in England and Wales
Chartered Accountants Hall
Moorgate Place
London EC2P 2BJ

Tel: (0171) 628 7060

Institute of Directors
116 Pall Mall
London SW1Y 5ED

Tel: (0171) 839 1233

Local Enterprise Agencies
There are some 300 Local Enterprise agencies set up nationwide to encourage small businesses to start, grow and flourish. Contact them via your local reference library or speak to *Business in the Community* (see above).

National Association of Shopkeepers
Lynch House
91 Mansfield Road
Nottingham NG1 3FN

Tel: (0115) 947 5046

National Federation of Self-Employed & Small Businesses
32 St Anne's Road West
Lytham St Annes
Lancashire FY8 1NY

Tel: (01253) 720911

Office of the Data Protection Registrar
Wycliffe House
Water Lane
Wilmslow
Cheshire SK9 5AF

Tel: (01625) 535777

Patent Office
25 Southampton Buildings
Chancery Lane
London WC2A 1AY

Tel: (0171) 438 4700

Small Firms Service
Local centres throughout the country. Phone free for local address:

Tel: (0800) 222999

The Trademarks Registry
25 Southampton Buildings
Chancery Lane
London WC2A 1AY

Tel: (0171) 438 4700

Index

HOW TO EMPLOY & MANAGE STAFF
A practical handbook for managers and supervisors

Wendy Wyatt

Now in a revised second edition, this easy to use handbook is intended for all young managers, supervisors and students whose work will involve them in recruiting and managing staff. Ideal for quick reference, it provides a ready-made framework of modern employment practice from recruitment onwards. It provides a clear account of how to apply the health & safety at work regulations, how to handle record-keeping, staff development, grievance and disciplinary procedures, maternity and sick leave and similar matters for the benefit of the organisation and its employees. The book includes a useful summary of current employment legislation and is complete with a range of model forms, letters, notices and similar documents. Wendy Wyatt MIPD is a Personnel Management and Employment Consultant; her other books include *Recruiting Success* and *Jobhunt*.

176pp illus. 1 85703 167 9. 2nd edition.

HOW TO MANAGE AN OFFICE
Creating and managing a successful workplace

Ann Dobson

Good office management is one of the keys to success in any organisation. The benefits are a happy and productive staff, satisfied customers, and a sound base from which to tackle such issues as growth and change within the organisation. Written by an experienced office manager and business consultant, this book suggests a complete practical framework for the well run office. It discusses what an office is for, the office as communications, the office as workplace, equipment, hygiene, health and security, external appearances, managing visitors, handling orders and information, managing office supplies, the office budget, staff management, and managing an office move.

160pp illus. 1 85703 049 4.

MANAGING MEETINGS
How to prepare, how to take part and how to follow up

Ann Dobson

Meetings can be interesting, productive and even fun! That is the message this new 'How To' book seeks to convey. Meetings form a large part of our lives today, particularly in the business world, yet many of us feel ill equipped to handle them with ease. The book is divided into two parts: the first covers the key skills of communicating effectively, motivating and persuading, problem solving, decision making, body language, and dealing with troublemakers. Part 2 deals with the practical steps of holding a meeting and following up. Case studies, self-assessment material and checklists complete the simple, yet effective approach. Ann Dobson is Principal of a Secretarial Training School, and has been involved with meetings of varying types for many years. She is also the author of *How to Communicate at Work, How to Write Business Letters, How to Return to Work* and *How to Manage an Office* in this series.

128pp illus. 1 85703 222 5.

MANAGING YOURSELF
How to achieve your personal goals in life and at work

Julie-Ann Amos

Managing yourself is often more difficult than it seems. So many other people, events and things seem to take control of, exert influence over, or just interfere with our lives and how we want to behave. This simple book goes beyond assertiveness and behaviour, and examines how to deal *inside* ourselves with the daily conflicts of everyday life. The reader will learn how to handle criticism, thoughts and emotions, aggression, passivity, change, conflict, and stress, through developing assertive communications and listening skills, body language and confidence. Julie-Ann Amos is a Member of the Institute of Personnel and Development. She is a Senior Personnel Officer and Trainer with a large local authority, and has taught Assertiveness and Personal Effectiveness programmes for many years. She has post-graduate qualifications in both Personnel and Administrative Management.

160pp illus. 1 85703 324 8.

HOW TO MASTER BOOK-KEEPING
A practical step-by-step guide

Peter Marshall

Illustrated at every stage with specimen entries, the book will be an ideal companion for students taking LCCI, RSA, BTEC, accountancy technician and similar courses at schools, colleges or training centres. Typical business transactions are used to illustrate all the essential theory, practice and skills required to be effective in a real business setting. 'Has a number of welcome and unusual features... The content is broken down into mind-sized chunks and the treatment is generally friendly.' *School Librarian journal.* 'An interesting approach.' *Association of Business Executives journal.* 'A complete step-by-step guide... each section of the book teaches a useful skill in its own right.' *OwnBase.* 'In addition to providing a useful approach to the teaching and learning of book-keeping skills, the way in which the text is presented should ensure that the book also provides a valuable reference source for revision and prompting.' *Teeline.*

176pp illus. 1 85703 065 6. 2nd edition.

HOW TO MANAGE PEOPLE AT WORK
A practical guide to effective leadership

John Humphries

'These days, if a textbook on people management is to succeed, it must be highly informative, reliable, comprehensive – and eminently user-friendly. Without doubt, *How to Manage People at Work* is one such book. Written in an attractive style that should appeal to any first-line manager who has neither the time nor the energy to cope with heavy reading, John Humphries has tackled his extremely wide subject ably and well. Rightly or wrongly, it has always been my experience that one has only to read the first couple of pages of any textbook on people management to discover whether or not the author enjoys an empathy with the people at the sharp end – and here is one author who, for my money, has passed the test with flying colours.' *Progress/NEBS Management Association.*

160pp illus. 1 85703 068 0. 2nd edition.

HOW TO USE THE INTERNET
A practical introduction for every computer user

Graham Jones

The fast-growing Internet is set to revolutionise personal and business communications across the globe, as well as entertainment, information and education. Unlike other books on 'The Net', here is a down to earth practical guide that will help you get the most out of this communication revolution. Gone are the heavy technical introductions, the in-depth computer instructions. Instead, here are simple, straightforward steps that anyone can use to get onto the Net and start exploring the new information super highway. Soon, nearly everyone in the developed world will have access to the Internet. This book shows you how and where to begin. Graham Jones is a leading business consultant and author. He is the author of *How to Manage Computers at Work* in this series, and has contributed to many computer magazines. He is Managing Director of a specialist business that utilises the Internet for up-to-date information.

126pp. illus. 1 85703 197 0.

HOW TO START YOUR OWN BUSINESS
Planning and creating a successful enterprise

Jim Green

This dynamic guide fully explores the vital steps to creating a business, interlaced with the author's recent experience in overcoming every hurdle encountered along the way in setting up his own business without capital or discretionary resources. It will show you how to galvanise into initial action, how to source proven ideas, how to write a winning plan, how to approach potential funders, how to present a case for public sector assistance, how to market your business and how to develop the selling habit. No matter what your age or personal circumstances, you *can* strike out on your own, create an enterprise and change your life for the better. Jim Green is chairman and managing director of Focus Publishing International Ltd and for many years specialised in founding, buying and selling advertising agencies.

159pp illus. 1 85703 122 9.

How To Books

How To Books provide practical help on a large range of topics. They are available through all good bookshops or can be ordered direct from the distributors. Just tick the titles you want and complete the form on the following page.

___ Apply to an Industrial Tribunal (£7.99)
___ Applying for a Job (£7.99)
___ Applying for a United States Visa (£15.99)
___ Be a Freelance Journalist (£8.99)
___ Be a Freelance Secretary (£8.99)
___ Be a Local Councillor (£8.99)
___ Be an Effective School Governor (£9.99)
___ Become a Freelance Sales Agent (£9.99)
___ Become an Au Pair (£8.99)
___ Buy & Run a Shop (£8.99)
___ Buy & Run a Small Hotel (£8.99)
___ Cash from your Computer (£9.99)
___ Career Planning for Women (£8.99)
___ Choosing a Nursing Home (£8.99)
___ Claim State Benefits (£9.99)
___ Communicate at Work (£7.99)
___ Conduct Staff Appraisals (£7.99)
___ Conducting Effective Interviews (£8.99)
___ Copyright & Law for Writers (£8.99)
___ Counsel People at Work (£7.99)
___ Creating a Twist in the Tale (£8.99)
___ Creative Writing (£9.99)
___ Critical Thinking for Students (£8.99)
___ Do Voluntary Work Abroad (£8.99)
___ Do Your Own Advertising (£8.99)
___ Do Your Own PR (£8.99)
___ Doing Business Abroad (£9.99)
___ Emigrate (£9.99)
___ Employ & Manage Staff (£8.99)
___ Find Temporary Work Abroad (£8.99)
___ Finding a Job in Canada (£9.99)
___ Finding a Job in Computers (£8.99)
___ Finding a Job in New Zealand (£9.99)
___ Finding a Job with a Future (£8.99)
___ Finding Work Overseas (£9.99)
___ Freelance DJ-ing (£8.99)
___ Get a Job Abroad (£10.99)
___ Get a Job in America (£9.99)
___ Get a Job in Australia (£9.99)
___ Get a Job in Europe (£9.99)
___ Get a Job in France (£9.99)
___ Get a Job in Germany (£9.99)
___ Get a Job in Hotels and Catering (£8.99)
___ Get a Job in Travel & Tourism (£8.99)
___ Get into Films & TV (£8.99)
___ Get into Radio (£8.99)
___ Get That Job (£6.99)
___ Getting your First Job (£8.99)
___ Going to University (£8.99)
___ Helping your Child to Read (£8.99)
___ Investing in People (£8.99)
___ Invest in Stocks & Shares (£8.99)

___ Keep Business Accounts (£7.99)
___ Know Your Rights at Work (£8.99)
___ Know Your Rights: Teachers (£6.99)
___ Live & Work in America (£9.99)
___ Live & Work in Australia (£12.99)
___ Live & Work in Germany (£9.99)
___ Live & Work in Greece (£9.99)
___ Live & Work in Italy (£8.99)
___ Live & Work in New Zealand (£9.99)
___ Live & Work in Portugal (£9.99)
___ Live & Work in Spain (£7.99)
___ Live & Work in the Gulf (£9.99)
___ Living & Working in Britain (£8.99)
___ Living & Working in China (£9.99)
___ Living & Working in Hong Kong (£10.99)
___ Living & Working in Israel (£10.99)
___ Living & Working in Japan (£8.99)
___ Living & Working in Saudi Arabia (£12.99)
___ Living & Working in the Netherlands (£9.99)
___ Lose Weight & Keep Fit (£6.99)
___ Make a Wedding Speech (£7.99)
___ Making a Complaint (£8.99)
___ Manage a Sales Team (£8.99)
___ Manage an Office (£8.99)
___ Manage Computers at Work (£8.99)
___ Manage People at Work (£8.99)
___ Manage Your Career (£8.99)
___ Managing Budgets & Cash Flows (£9.99)
___ Managing Meetings (£8.99)
___ Managing Your Personal Finances (£8.99)
___ Market Yourself (£8.99)
___ Master Book-Keeping (£8.99)
___ Mastering Business English (£8.99)
___ Master GCSE Accounts (£8.99)
___ Master Languages (£8.99)
___ Master Public Speaking (£8.99)
___ Obtaining Visas & Work Permits (£9.99)
___ Organising Effective Training (£9.99)
___ Pass Exams Without Anxiety (£7.99)
___ Pass That Interview (£6.99)
___ Plan a Wedding (£7.99)
___ Prepare a Business Plan (£8.99)
___ Publish a Book (£9.99)
___ Publish a Newsletter (£9.99)
___ Raise Funds & Sponsorship (£7.99)
___ Rent & Buy Property in France (£9.99)
___ Rent & Buy Property in Italy (£9.99)
___ Retire Abroad (£8.99)
___ Return to Work (£7.99)
___ Run a Local Campaign (£6.99)
___ Run a Voluntary Group (£8.99)
___ Sell Your Business (£9.99)

How To Books

___ Selling into Japan (£14.99)	___ Use the Internet (£9.99)
___ Setting up Home in Florida (£9.99)	___ Winning Consumer Competitions (£8.99)
___ Spend a Year Abroad (£8.99)	___ Winning Presentations (£8.99)
___ Start a Business from Home (£7.99)	___ Work from Home (£8.99)
___ Start a New Career (£6.99)	___ Work in an Office (£7.99)
___ Starting to Manage (£8.99)	___ Work in Retail (£8.99)
___ Starting to Write (£8.99)	___ Work with Dogs (£8.99)
___ Start Word Processing (£8.99)	___ Working Abroad (£14.99)
___ Start Your Own Business (£8.99)	___ Working as a Holiday Rep (£9.99)
___ Study Abroad (£8.99)	___ Working in Japan (£10.99)
___ Study & Learn (£7.99)	___ Working in Photography (£8.99)
___ Study & Live in Britain (£7.99)	___ Working in the Gulf (£10.99)
___ Studying at University (£8.99)	___ Working on Contract Worldwide (£9.99)
___ Studying for a Degree (£8.99)	___ Working on Cruise Ships (£9.99)
___ Successful Grandparenting (£8.99)	___ Write a CV that Works (£7.99)
___ Successful Mail Order Marketing (£9.99)	___ Write a Press Release (£9.99)
___ Successful Single Parenting (£8.99)	___ Write a Report (£8.99)
___ Survive at College (£4.99)	___ Write an Assignment (£8.99)
___ Survive Divorce (£8.99)	___ Write an Essay (£7.99)
___ Surviving Redundancy (£8.99)	___ Write & Sell Computer Software (£9.99)
___ Take Care of Your Heart (£5.99)	___ Write Business Letters (£8.99)
___ Taking in Students (£8.99)	___ Write for Publication (£8.99)
___ Taking on Staff (£8.99)	___ Write for Television (£8.99)
___ Taking Your A-Levels (£8.99)	___ Write Your Dissertation (£8.99)
___ Teach Abroad (£8.99)	___ Writing a Non Fiction Book (£8.99)
___ Teach Adults (£8.99)	___ Writing & Selling a Novel (£8.99)
___ Teaching Someone to Drive (£8.99)	___ Writing & Selling Short Stories (£8.99)
___ Travel Round the World (£8.99)	___ Writing Reviews (£8.99)
___ Use a Library (£6.99)	___ Your Own Business in Europe (£12.99)

To: Plymbridge Distributors Ltd, Plymbridge House, Estover Road, Plymouth PL6 7PZ.
Customer Services Tel: (01752) 202301. Fax: (01752) 202331.

Please send me copies of the titles I have indicated. Please add postage & packing
(UK £1, Europe including Eire, £2, World £3 airmail).

☐ I enclose cheque/PO payable to Plymbridge Distributors Ltd for £ [　　　　　]

☐ Please charge to my ☐ MasterCard, ☐ Visa, ☐AMEX card.

Account No. [ ][ ][ ][ ][ ][ ][ ][ ][ ][ ][ ][ ][ ][ ]

Card Expiry Date [ ][ ] 19 [ ] ☎ Credit Card orders may be faxed or phoned.

Customer Name (CAPITALS) ....

Address ....

.... Postcode..............

Telephone........................... Signature ....

Every effort will be made to despatch your copy as soon as possible but to avoid possible
disappointment please allow up to 21 days for despatch time (42 days if overseas). Prices
and availability are subject to change without notice.

[Code BPA]